Introduction to Cabin Crew

Beverley Goodman

Edited by Ray Youell

Published by Travel and Tourism Publishing Limited

www.tandtpublishing.co.uk
info@tandtpublishing.co.uk

First published 2015

British Library Cataloguing in Publication Data is available from the British Library on request.
ISBN 978-0-9576284-2-7

Copyright notice

Acknowledgements

Thank you to my family and friends, especially Chris, Stephen and Yolande, who have encouraged, critiqued and kept me focused. Thanks to Travel and Tourism Publishing, especially Ray Youell, for their input and advice.

Beverley Goodman

The publishers extend thanks to the following for granting permission to reproduce images throughout this book – Air Berlin, British Airways, Emirates, Virgin Atlantic, Wizzair, easyJet, Thomson Airways, Swissport, Etihad, Icelandair, Jet2, Qatar Airways, Malaysia Airlines, Seat Guru.

How to use this book

The purpose of this book is to develop your knowledge and understanding of the role of airline cabin crew. It seeks to dispel myths, to be informative and to encourage you to achieve your personal goals.

The book is structured around the 6 compulsory Units of the **Level 2 Introduction to Cabin Crew Qualification** offered by a number of awarding bodies (exam boards). Currently, these include Edexcel/BTEC, NCFE, City & Guilds and Ascentis. The book is designed to be relevant to a variety of other cabin crew training and education courses. It is a useful revision tool and will prove helpful when completing tests, assignments and interviews.

The *Level 2 Introduction to Cabin Crew Qualification* has been developed to give students the opportunity to:

- Engage in learning that is relevant to them and which will provide opportunities to develop a range of skills and techniques, personal skills and attributes essential for successful performance in working life
- Achieve a nationally-recognised Level 2 qualification
- Progress to employment in the airline industry

Each unit in this book includes:

- **An introductory page** – giving an overview of the content of the unit

- **A overview table** – showing the learning outcomes and assessment criteria for the unit

- **Clearly-labelled sections** – covering the specification content for the unit

- **Activities** – based on the assessment criteria to help you learn more

- **'Did you know?' sections** – short, practical examples of key facts related to the unit

- **Discussion points** – to help you understand main topics

- **Weblinks** – internet links to organisations and topics in the unit

At the end of the book is a **glossary** of common terms used by air cabin crew.

Teaching resources

To accompany this book, the author has developed very comprehensive resources and materials for teachers and lecturers who are delivering the *Level 2 Introduction to Cabin Crew Qualification*. These include detailed schemes of work, student activities with answers, PowerPoint® presentations, assignment briefs, airline-specific paperwork, links to useful websites, etc.

You can find full details of these teaching resources and download sample pages from our website www.tandtpublishing.co.uk.

About the author

Before embarking on a successful teaching career, Beverley Goodman worked as a member of cabin crew for the UK's largest charter airline. Achieving her personal ambition to become cabin crew, she progressed from a junior role to recruiting, training and managing other cabin crew for the 12 years she was with the company. This wealth of experience provided an excellent foundation for 20 years of teaching vocational travel and tourism courses at the largest Further Education College in Bedfordshire. Throughout the delivery of the cabin crew courses, support from a local airline ensured knowledge and procedural updates in line with industry developments. It also gave her students the opportunity to experience a realistic working environment in their mock cabin facility. Although recently retired from teaching, Beverley's driving force continues to revolve around sharing knowledge, providing information, nurturing aspirations and a lifelong passion for the travel industry.

Level 2 Introduction to Cabin Crew

Table of contents

Acknowledgements ii
How to use this book and details of teaching resources iii
About the author iv

Unit 1: Working as cabin crew   **1**

1) Roles and responsibilities of cabin crew   3
2) Aviation terminology used by cabin crew   7
3) Pre and post-flight duties   9
4) Pre-flight briefing   10
5) Maintaining industry standards   11

Unit 2: Airline health, safety and security   **13**

1) Airline health and safety documentation and legislation   15
2) The role of cabin crew in ensuring safety and security   23
3) Maintaining passenger compliance   26
4) Dealing with medical issues   28

Unit 3: Aircraft emergency situations   **33**

1) Understand how to respond to aircraft emergencies   35
2) Knowing on-board emergency procedures   41
3) Following on-board emergency procedures   46
4) Primary principles for survival after an airline emergency   47

Unit 4: Dealing with passengers on board an aircraft   **49**

1) Passengers with special requirements   51
2) Providing effective customer service   53
3) Dealing with passenger problems and complaints   55
4) How to work as part of a team   55
5) Handling incidents and conflict situations   57
6) Being able to deal with passengers   59

Unit 5: Cabin service – selling techniques   **61**

1) Establishing rapport with passengers   63
2) Establishing passenger needs and wants   64
3) On-board products and services   66
4) Selling techniques   72
5) Currency calculations   73
6) Providing a cabin service   75

Level 2 Introduction to Cabin Crew

Unit 6: Making passenger announcements on board an aircraft — 77

    1) Know how to use passenger announcements during a flight — 78
    2) Be able to make passenger announcements — 83

Glossary — 85

Level 2 Introduction to Cabin Crew

Working as cabin crew

Introduction

When people ask you what job you do and you reply "*I'm cabin crew*" their faces light up. They imagine a glamorous job, lots of worldwide travel and exciting opportunities. What they do not always appreciate is the responsibility and the hard work that is involved.

The primary role of airline cabin crew is to ensure the safety, health and welfare of their passengers.

At 35,000 feet there is no opportunity to dial 999 if a fire breaks out – *you* are the firefighter. There's no paramedic or ambulance if someone has a heart attack or threatens a miscarriage – *you* have to deal with the medical emergency. If someone becomes aggressive and abusive can you call the police? No, *you* must deal with it. Who supports and gives advice to passengers in an emergency situation? Yes it's *you.*

You welcome your 'guests' on to the aircraft. Each person wants individual attention, but *you* will be on your feet for hours and, throughout the flight, *you* will be entertaining, serving and communicating with your guests. *You* represent the company and it's up to *you* to reassure anyone who is nervous. *You* identify individual needs and *you* increase company revenue through the sale of on-board products. *You* say "g*oodbye*" at the end of the flight and then, after a short turnaround, *you* will repeat the process.

Is this the career for *you*? Yes – if you like being with people, enjoy challenges and want every day to be different – being cabin crew is the job for you.

This unit will help you to develop your knowledge and understanding of:

- The roles and responsibilities of air cabin crew
- The chain of command on the aircraft
- The ground staff that cabin crew interact with
- Industry-specific terminology
- IATA codes
- Pre and post-flight briefings
- Industry standards related to time keeping, personal grooming and uniform
- Task prioritisation
- Customer service

Learning Outcomes	Assessment Criteria
1 Know the roles and responsibilities of crew	**1.1** Outline the different roles cabin crew may have to undertake **1.2** Describe the responsibilities associated with the cabin crew roles **1.3** Identify the chain of command on an aircraft **1.4** Describe the roles of ground staff that cabin crew will interact with
2 Know aviation terminology used by cabin crew	**2.1** Identify IATA (International Air Transport Association) codes that are used by airlines and airports nationally and internationally **2.2** Define key industry terms **2.3** Describe the different types of duties cabin crew may be scheduled to undertake, including different types of standby
3 Know the pre and post-flight duties that cabin crew undertake in the crew room	**3.1** Describe the duties undertaken by cabin crew before the pre-flight briefing **3.2** Describe the importance of time keeping prior to a pre-flight briefing **3.3** Identify the elements of a pre-flight briefing **3.4** Identify the elements of post-flight briefing
4 Be able to take part in a pre-flight briefing	**4.1** Receive and relay Safety and Emergency Procedures (SEP) information during a pre-flight briefing **4.2** Complete documentation relating to a pre-flight briefing in readiness for the flight
5 Understand the importance of maintaining industry standards	**5.1** Explain the importance of time keeping **5.2** Explain the importance of grooming and uniform standards **5.3** Describe personal presentation standards on and off duty and during stopovers **5.4** Explain the importance of task management and prioritisation of tasks **5.5** Explain the importance of customer relationship management (CRM)

1. Roles and responsibilities of cabin crew

Each crew member will have set procedures to follow before the passengers board the aircraft. The number of cabin crew members on each flight depends on the type of flight, the size of the aircraft and the service requirements.

> **Did you know?** For every 50 passengers on board an aircraft there needs to be a minimum of 1 cabin crew member. This is a legal CAA (Civil Aviation Authority) requirement.

Activity →

Visit www.seatguru.com and look at a range of aircraft configurations (types). What is the difference between narrow and wide-bodied aircraft?

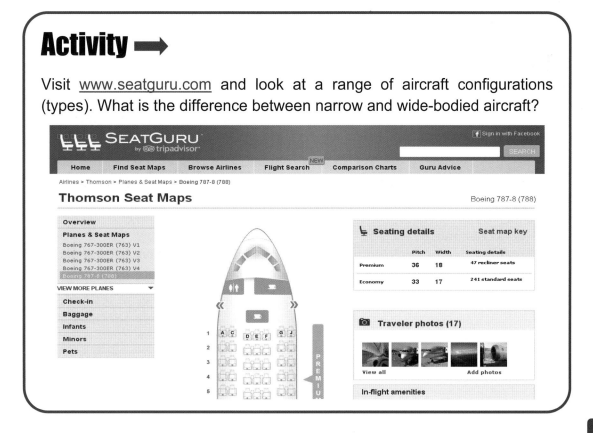

3

Routine procedures

When the cabin crew first board the aircraft they complete a variety of checks. It is important to do this first so that any faulty or missing equipment can be replaced or mended before the passengers board the aircraft.

Emergency checks are completed before every flight so that, if an emergency situation occurs, the cabin crew would have the necessary items to deal with it. Some of the checks are security-focused to ensure suspect items have not been placed on board the aircraft. Other checks are related to passenger welfare, for example testing the communication system, toilets, in-flight entertainment and galley (catering) equipment.

Once the checks and preparations have been completed the cabin crew move to their designated boarding positions, where they will meet and greet the passengers.

Discussion Point ⟷
Why is it important for cabin crew to welcome their passengers on board?

Cabin crew members must complete a head count to check passenger numbers and confirm these to the senior member of cabin crew, known as the Customer Service Manager/Flight Director/Purser/No.1. When counting passengers the best method is to actually count heads rather than empty seats. If a child under 2 is travelling then they are expressed as +1 (plus one). For example, on a flight with one hundred and twenty nine passengers and six children the total on board will be 129+6. After the Captain has confirmed that the departure preparations have been completed and the ground handling staff have left the aircraft, the cabin crew close the aircraft doors. As soon as the aircraft doors are closed the 'arming' process takes place.

Did you know? When cabin crew talk about 'arming' a door, they mean that the escape slide is now ready to be used when the door is opened should an emergency evacuation be needed.

The aircraft will now taxi towards the runway for take-off while the cabin crew deliver the safety demonstration, which includes information on the location of emergency exits, the use of life jackets and seatbelt procedures. Much of this information is also included in the safety card found on each passenger's seat back.

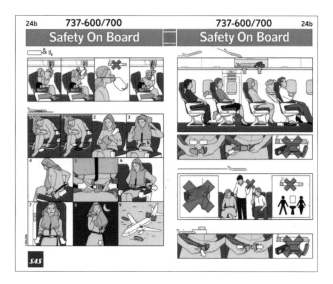

Members of cabin crew then complete the pre-take off seatbelt checks on the passengers, inform the flight crew that the cabin is secure and return to their jump seats and secure their own seat belts.

Did you know? The crew seats are located adjacent to main emergency exit routes. These seats are referred to as 'jump seats' because they flip up (like a cinema seat) to make sure emergency exit routes are free from obstructions at all times.

In-flight duties usually start once the 'fasten seatbelt' sign has been switched off. The order of service will depend on the length and type of flight. For example, on an early morning flight, which is catered with breakfast, the crew will postpone the drinks service until later.

Level 2 Introduction to Cabin Crew

Pre-landing checks involve preparing the aircraft and passengers for landing at the destination. The cabin crew make sure that all equipment and luggage is secured in the correct areas, passenger seat backs and seat tables are in the upright position, window blinds are open and the toilets locked.

When the aircraft arrives on its allocated stand (the parking area) outside the terminal building and the engines have been switched off, the command for disarming the aircraft doors will be given by the flight crew. Once the fasten seatbelt signs are switched off, passengers can safely leave the aircraft.

> **Did you know?** As a passenger you may hear the announcement "cabin crew prepare the doors" or "cabin crew doors to manual". This is the instruction to the cabin crew to disarm/disengage the evacuation slide so that the aircraft door(s) can be opened for passengers to disembark via an air bridge or steps.

Chain of command on aircraft

On board the aircraft all members of cabin crew work as a team. However, to ensure that the flight is efficient and well-organised each member of the team will have a specific crew position, duties and responsibilities. The ultimate responsibility for decision making on board the aircraft rests with the Captain – any decisions relating to the safety, security or welfare of the passengers must be referred to him or her.

If the Captain becomes unwell or incapacitated in any way, the next in command is the co-pilot, sometimes referred to as the First Officer.

In the passenger cabin the senior member of cabin crew has the authority to make decisions related to service matters and customer care. If the situation is safety or security related then it must be referred to the Captain for his/her decision.

This chain of command is generic to all aircraft types and the length of the chain will depend on the number of cabin crew and flight crew on board. Long-haul flights on larger planes need more staff than short-haul trips. Junior members report to the next senior member immediately above them – this is known as line management.

Ground staff and cabin crew interaction

While on the ground, cabin crew interact with a number of different airport personnel. Some of these work for the same company as the cabin crew, e.g. operations staff, crewing, cashiers and base managers.

Other personnel work for support companies and are key in getting the aircraft ready for the flight, for example engineers, aircraft cleaners, catering and bar carts loaders as well as ground handling staff, e.g. passenger service agents and aircraft dispatchers.

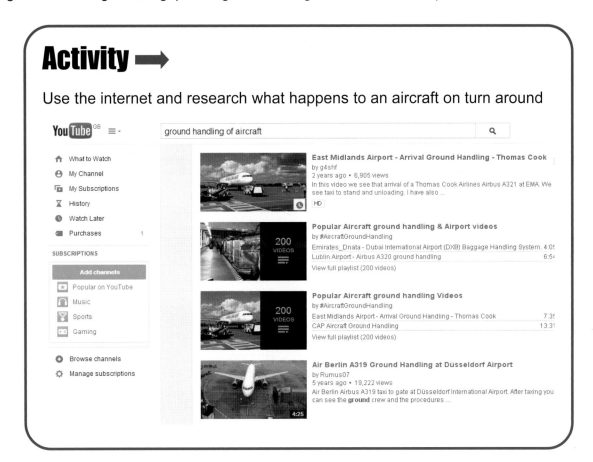

2. Aviation terminology used by cabin crew

When you work at an airport, either on the ground or in the air, there is a whole new language to learn. The terms are used frequently by many people working in the airline industry, including passenger service agents, aircraft dispatchers and flight crew, so it is vital

© 2015 Travel & Tourism Publishing Ltd   Level 2 Introduction to Cabin Crew

for the smooth operation of the airline business that the terminology is understood by everyone.

English is the universal language used by the worldwide aviation industry. However, cabin crew are required to learn airline specific terminology and express these using the phonetic alphabet. This alphabet was introduced in the 1950s by NATO to standardise the words used to describe the letters of the alphabet. The phonetic alphabet has now become the accepted means of spelling out names, abbreviations and aircraft registrations. Once you have learnt it you will find you use it often.

A	Alpha	**J**	Juliet	**S**	Sierra
B	Bravo	**K**	Kilo	**T**	Tango
C	Charlie	**L**	Lima	**U**	Uniform
D	Delta	**M**	Mike	**V**	Victor
E	Echo	**N**	November	**W**	Whiskey
F	Foxtrot	**O**	Oscar	**X**	X-ray
G	Golf	**P**	Papa	**Y**	Yankee
H	Hotel	**Q**	Quebec	**Z**	Zulu
I	India	**R**	Romeo		

IATA (the International Air Transport Association) is an international organisation which is responsible for allocating codes for airlines, cities and airports. They also issue codes for meals and passenger types.

As cabin crew you will become familiar with the 3-letter codes used for the main UK airports. Some codes are easily recognisable, e.g. EDI – Edinburgh and LBA – Leeds Bradford, while others are less obvious, e.g. Cardiff – CWL and Birmingham – BHX. Airlines use 2-letter codes to identify the company, for example BA – British Airways and MT – Thomas Cook. These letters usually precede numbers and are used to compile the flight numbers found on all documentation relating to a flight, as shown in the following example from Virgin Atlantic.

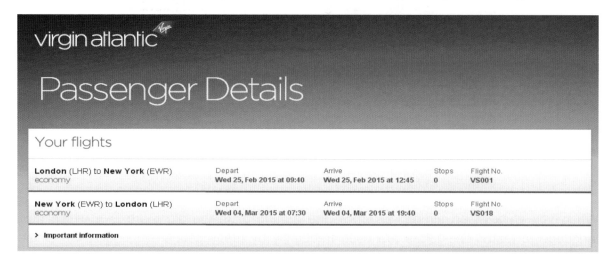

Level 2 Introduction to Cabin Crew

Cabin crew need to be aware of the range of codes used for meals, passenger types and medical conditions. These are used on a range of documents related to flight information.

Airline terminology is used widely throughout the industry and it is important to learn key phrases, e.g. airside, landside, bulkhead, chocks, etc. See the glossary on page 85 for more key terms used by cabin crew.

Abbreviations are often used in documents, such as flight reports and pre-flight briefings. Cabin crew use the abbreviations when talking and it is important to know what they mean. The following table shows some common examples.

A/C	Aircraft	**I/B**	Inbound
Pap (Pax)	Passenger(s)	**OPS**	Operations
ATA	Actual time of arrival	**SEP**	Safety and Emergency Procedures
ETA	Estimated time of arrival	**SNY**	Supernumerary
ATC	Air traffic control	**TBA**	To be advised
O/B	Outbound	**U/S**	Unserviceable

3.   Pre and post-flight duties

Cabin crew generally know which flights they will be operating at least a month in advance. The document that gives them this information is known as their 'roster'. Most airlines deliver the information electronically while some produce a paper version. The roster covers a certain period of time and gives details of the flight operation, including the time of the flight and the crew position you will be operating in. Below is a section from a roster.

Date	Outbound Flight	Inbound Flight
TUE 08 SEP 15	21.21 LTN – ACE 01.36	02.59 ACE– LGW 07.42
WED 09 SEP 15		
THU 10 SEP 15	06.00 LTN – AGP 08.30	09.30 AGP – LTN 12.30
FRI 11 SEP 15	06.20 LTN – MXP 08.20	09.40 MXP – LTN 12.10
SAT 12 SEP 15	08.00 LTN – ALC 10.30	11.30 ALC – LTN 14.02

> ## Activity ➡
>
> Use the website www.world-airport-codes.com to see which airports the cabin crew member whose roster is shown on page 9 will be visiting.

The cabin crew use their roster to work out their time to report for duty. Most airlines stipulate that cabin crew must arrive 1 hour 30 minutes before take-off. During this period of time they will:

- Check for any roster changes
- Make a note of crew names
- Read health, safety and security notices
- Collect paperwork and bar floats
- Obtain information about any specific passenger needs and requirements
- Sign in (this process confirms that they are rested, fit to work and have read all crew notices)
- Go to the briefing area
- Introduce themselves to the other crew members and attend the pre-flight briefing

4.   Pre-flight briefing

The pre-flight briefing is an important element of flight preparations. It is an opportunity to establish a good working relationship and share information, and therefore it is vital that all crew members are punctual and prepared.

The senior member of cabin crew is in charge of the process and is responsible for:

- Introducing crew members and confirming flight details
- Delegating crew positions (consideration will be given to seniority, experience and service requirements)
- Ensuring that the cabin crew appearance is to the company standard
- Informing crew of the order of service (bar, meals, sales) for the flight
- Checking that all crew have read the notices and understand any new procedures
- Ask SEP questions (one safety related, one first-aid and one security)
- Motivating and co-ordinating the team

The crew will then go out to the aircraft to prepare for passenger arrival.

Level 2 Introduction to Cabin Crew

The post-flight briefing is probably the next opportunity the crew will all be together in the same room. At the end of the flight the crew will return to the crew room to:

- Count the money taken on the flight
- Complete bar paperwork
- Complete the flight report, including any incidents or feedback the company will need
- Take part in a flight evaluation
- Give feedback to individual crew members
- Say "*thank you*" and "*goodbye*"

5.   Maintaining industry standards

As cabin crew it is vital to maintain the highest industry standards at all times. An airline's reputation could be influenced by the experience a passenger has at any stage of their journey. As cabin crew you will need to:

- Be organised
- Be punctual
- Maintain personal presentation
- Behave appropriately
- Be professional at all times

All members of cabin crew must:

- Understand routine and non-routine tasks
- Prioritise tasks in order of importance
- Prioritise tasks, taking into consideration legal and regulatory requirements

Customer relationship management (CRM) is a key aspect of the training programme for cabin crew. Part of the training for new recruits is how to deliver excellent customer service. Passengers judge an airline on the personal experience they receive and their interaction with cabin crew.

The starting point for each airline is to develop their service standards and procedures, train their staff to deliver them and constantly review and monitor their performance. For cabin crew, CRM standards are part of their personal assessment and for a new recruit comments made about their skills could be the deciding factor when permanent contracts are offered. For established cabin crew, flight report feedback on CRM performance could affect promotion opportunities.

CRM is also important to the reputation of the airline. Passengers expect consistency in terms of service and will compare one airline against another. Therefore it is important for the cabin crew to work as a team following company procedures and maintaining industry standards, ensuring passengers' welfare…. But how do *you* make the flight experience memorable? How will *you* go that extra mile?

Activity ➡

Be the passenger! Produce a list of what would make your flight exceptional (be realistic). One inspirational idea is the Virgin Atlantic Ice Cream Story – use the internet to find out about this idea and discuss why the decision was important to the company.

Why is CRM important to an airline? The system helps to:

- Retain customers
- Reward loyal customers
- Attract new customers
- Motivate staff
- Maintain reputation
- Ensure customer welfare

When passengers are asked for comments about their flight they may comment on leg room, in-flight entertainment or the quality of the meal they received. But, mostly they comment on the attentiveness of the cabin crew, the friendly approach, the welcome and the service they receive. Yes, *you* are there for passenger safety; *you* are there to deal with health issues; *you* are looking after the passenger's welfare, but on the majority of flights there will not be any problems; *you* are there to make the journey enjoyable, memorable and stress-free.

02 Airline health, safety and security

Introduction

All members of cabin crew need to be aware of, and understand the significance of, certain government regulations and legislation. Remember you are on board for the health, safety and wellbeing of your passengers, as well as having a responsibility to safeguard company equipment and ensure you do not endanger your colleagues.

It is not essential to study the regulations and legislation in detail, but you do need to have an awareness of why they are in place and your responsibility to maintain them.

You will also have the opportunity to demonstrate your skills in performing a safety demonstration and undertaking cabin secure checks, both of which are essential duties of air cabin crew.

This unit will help you to develop your knowledge and understanding of:

- Airline industry standards of health, safety and security

- Industry regulations and legislation

- Documents used to record incidents related to health and safety

- The role of cabin crew in making sure procedures are followed pre-flight, during the flight and post-flight to maintain a healthy, safe and secure environment

- The practical skills necessary to perform a safety demonstration

- Cabin secure checks

- On-board medical issues and how to deal with them

Learning Outcomes	Assessment Criteria
1 Know airline health and safety documentation and legislation	**1.1** Outline current legislation and regulations related to airline health and safety **1.2** Identify key points of the Air Navigation Order (ANO) used to protect the health and safety of the airline's crew, aircraft and passengers **1.3** Identify documents airlines use to record health and safety events on board an aircraft
2 Understand the role of cabin crew in ensuring the safety and security of passengers and crew	**2.1** Outline the key points of the legislation relating to aviation security **2.2** Describe security measures taken pre-flight, in-flight and post-flight **2.3** Identify restricted articles and dangerous items **2.4** Describe types of threat that relate to the aviation industry **2.5** Explain the procedures for dealing with on-board security incidents **2.6** Explain the importance of checking passenger boarding cards in relation to security
3 Be able to maintain passenger compliance	**3.1** Perform a safety demonstration **3.2** Carry out cabin secure checks
4 Understand how medical issues are dealt with by cabin crew	**4.1** Describe passenger signs and symptoms of minor and serious medical issues **4.2** Describe passenger treatment of minor and serious medical issues **4.3** Identify restrictions crew face on board when giving first-aid **4.4** Describe the types of on board first-aid kits **4.5** State which external bodies are able to assist crew during and after a first-aid situation

1. Airline health and safety documentation and legislation

Health and safety legislation and regulations

IATA regulations

IATA (the International Air Transport Association) interacts with airline companies and associated businesses worldwide on many aspects of air travel, for example 3-letter airport codes. IATA is also responsible for updating and informing the aviation industry about a range of policies, procedures and recommendations to do with health and safety.

One aspect of their work relates to 'dangerous goods', which are substances and equipment used on board the aircraft that could cause damage to health, property or the surrounding environment.

> **Did you know?** Some of the equipment that may be used in a medical situation could be classified as 'dangerous goods'. The airline, however, will have written permission from the authority to have these items on board and cabin staff will be trained in how to use them and checked on their knowledge on a regular basis.

Members of cabin crew also receive training about the transport of dangerous goods, prohibited (forbidden) items and the procedure for dealing with any in-flight leakage or spillage of these items.

IATA and the CAA (Civil Aviation Authority) keep airlines updated with any new developments and changes to procedures. Airlines pass this information on to their staff through training or an internal SEP (Safety and Emergency Procedures) communication.

> **Activity** ➡
>
> Search the official UK government website (www.gov.uk) for information on hand luggage that can be taken on to an aircraft. Study the section that covers 'chemicals and toxic substances'. Can you think of any circumstances when *you*, as a passenger, might take one of the listed items? Discuss the consequences of this.

Health and Safety at Work Act 1974

This legislation is in place to promote the safety, health and welfare of people at work. It also protects others against risks to health and safety. Employers have a duty of care to employees and visitors to their premises. Employees also have a responsibility to inform employers of any risks or hazards that they may observe in their working environment. Employers must keep their staff informed of any changes to procedures, update working practices and ensure a training schedule is in place. In an airline the CAA monitors these training programmes, all flight reports and incident records, as well as investigating any accidents. If any changes need to be made, the CAA will inform the airline and then monitor the process.

The Health and Safety at Work Act 1974 is an important piece of legislation. All **employers** must be aware of the consequences of not having adequate procedures and training in place. As an **employee** you must be aware of your personal responsibilities to your employer, colleagues and passengers. All employers have to have the relevant Health and Safety Executive (HSE) poster on display in the workplace or to give each of their employees a leaflet/pocket card about the legislation. The information is written in basic language and must be available to all employees. Translations into languages other than English are available.

In the aircraft, the cabin crew are responsible for maintaining health and safety – not only of the passengers, but of their colleagues as well, e.g. leaving a pot of boiling liquid on the edge of a work surface is not considered 'safe'. Cabin crew need to consider 'risk and outcome' in their everyday duties, while being vigilant and responsible at all times. If a situation occurs, this needs to be reported back to the company via the flight report. For example, if you spilt coffee over a passenger because the pot handle was slippery, the equipment may need to be modified. If you spilt coffee because the aircraft unexpectedly hit turbulence, then the method of serving coffee may need to be changed.

Airlines establish guidelines and inform cabin crew of these during their initial and ongoing training, e.g. alcohol consumption, medication and sufficient rest can all have an impact on an individual's performance while at work.

COSHH Regulations 2002 (Control of Substances Hazardous to Health)

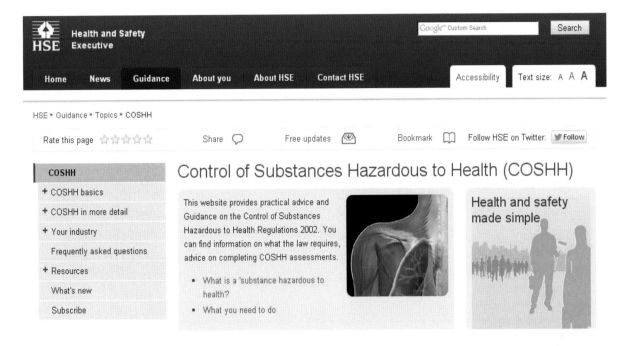

Employers are required by law to identify substances that may be a health hazard and put preventative measures in place to protect their employees, visitors and customers. The COSHH Regulations place a duty on employers to:

1. Identify any health hazards
2. Complete a risk assessment, which will help to identify how to prevent harm to health
3. Provide training and guidance to ensure that everyone is made aware of the hazards and how to avoid them
4. Make sure that everybody follows the guidelines

Employers have a duty of care to ensure all control measures are in good working order. They must provide information and training for employees on a regular basis and have a system in place to notify them of changes to procedures. Within the workplace, there needs to be a system to monitor procedures and a plan for emergencies.

One of the basic procedures is to provide personal protective equipment (PPE) for employees. The COSHH Regulations state that it is the employer's responsibility to provide, replace and pay for any PPE that is needed.

Did you know? Some items of PPE may be used frequently by cabin crew, e.g. disposable gloves and high visibility jackets. Other items are used less frequently, for example resuscitation masks (for mouth-to-mouth resuscitation) or an eye bath and solution.

Manual Handling Operations Regulations 1992

These Regulations require employers to inform and train employees about the safe handling and lifting of items in the workplace, so as to reduce the risk of injury. Manual handling is described as moving or supporting a load, including lifting, sitting down, pulling or pushing, carrying or moving, by hand or bodily force. Employees are expected to take personal responsibility for safe lifting and manual handling.

> **Did you know?** It is not only a person's back that can be injured by poor manual handling. As a member of cabin crew, there are many instances when you may be at risk of injury, e.g. pushing a loaded bar cart up to the front of the aircraft while it is still climbing to cruise altitude can put a strain on your back and legs. In this case, cabin crew will be advised to work together – one pulling and the other pushing – to minimise the risks.

Health, Safety and Welfare Regulations 1992

These Regulations were introduced to ensure the protection of everyone in the workplace and to make sure that welfare facilities are provided. They also:

- Cover the needs of people with disabilities – the provision for the workforce must be 'suitable' and this could mean making changes to work stations, access and transit routes as well as toilet provision

- Contain guidance about ventilation, temperature in indoor workplaces, hot and cold environments, lighting, cleanliness and waste materials plus room dimensions, space, workstations and seating

Disability Discrimination Act (DDA) 1995

This Act of Parliament makes it unlawful to discriminate against people because of a disability they may have. This law relates to employment, the provision of goods and services, education and transport. Employers can still have reasonable medical criteria for employment and they can expect satisfactory work standards from employees once reasonable adjustments have been made. The same legislation also states that organisations must make reasonable adjustments to ensure that people with disabilities have access to their services and transport.

> **Did you know?** Not all disabilities are immediately visible and some disabilities may impact upon the types of employment you are seeking. Working at altitude, in a confined space, for long duty periods and with no regular sleep pattern can affect a number of medical conditions, which people can manage successfully on the ground, e.g. diabetes, but would be unable to manage if employed as cabin crew.

Food Hygiene Regulations 1996

These Regulations give guidance on handling and processing food that is for human consumption. They also set out standards for food storage, packaging and ingredients.

It is important that cabin crew have an awareness of the need to re-heat meals to the required temperature, ensure certain items are kept chilled and that, when serving meals, hygiene standards are maintained at all times.

Basic hygiene practices, e.g. frequently washing hands, wiping down surfaces thoroughly and using probes to test food temperature, are essential. When dealing with situations such as the disposal of a sick bag, disposable gloves must be used to maintain hygiene standards and minimise health risks.

> **Did you know?** When cabin crew are on overseas stopovers in certain countries, they are given guidance about food to avoid, e.g. shellfish, and only drinking water from sealed bottles and not using ice to cool drinks. On the flight, the Captain and First Officer never eat the same meal and the cabin crew will have a choice of meals to ensure that the risk of food poisoning is minimised.

EU Ops

As commercial air travel developed, it became essential to establish guidelines and working practices for aircraft operations. Airlines must have an Air Operator Certificate and an Operator's Licence to offer flights for passengers. JAR Ops (Joint Aviation Requirements) became the standard and provided guidelines of the requirements that airlines had to work to.

In July 2008 EU Ops was established. This document is effective in all EU (European Union) states, plus Norway, Switzerland and Iceland.

> **Did you know?** There are a number of different sections within EU Ops, which are incorporated into the development of company operations manuals, e.g. sub-section O relates to cabin crew, sub-section P to manuals, logs and records and sub-section Q to flight and duty time restrictions and rest requirements. These operations manuals are regularly checked by the CAA to ensure they are accurate and current.

Air Navigation Order (ANO)

The Air Navigation Order contains information about the day-to-day operation of the aviation industry. The focus of the CAA is to ensure safe air travel and they use legislation (international, European and domestic) to update and produce the ANO. This publication sets the standards for recruitment, training and procedures within all aspects of the aviation industry.

Health and safety documentation

As an employer of an 'absent' workforce, where much of the work is carried out away from the company base, it is important that airlines have a system of communication which captures and reports incidents. All airlines have these systems in place, some of which will remain on board the aircraft and relate only to that particular aircraft, and other documents which are completed routinely by the crew and returned to the company.

> **Did you know?** Each aircraft has its own registration number which is issued by IATA (the International Air Transport Association) and incorporates a country code (G for the UK) and four letters. All documents that are completed use this aircraft registration, dates, flight route, etc.

Flight report

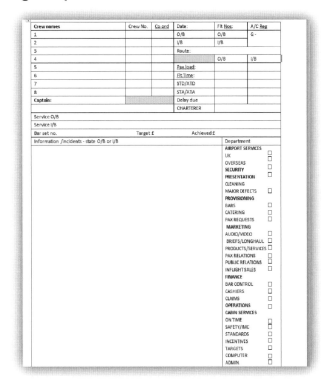

A flight report is completed for each flight. It contains details of the operating crew, the Captain's name, dates and flight details, aircraft registration and a record of what occurred on the flight.

The flight report is returned to base where it will be read and any necessary actions will be processed, e.g. a passenger returning in 2 weeks requires a vegetarian meal.

The flight report is a legal document and in certain circumstances may be accessed by the CAA. The report must be signed and dated.

Did you know? Some airlines use electronic flight report systems, but the principle remains the same and details must be completed accurately, in a factual and informative style. The report must be submitted at the end of the flight (or if operating overseas at the first possible opportunity). It should be signed and dated by the senior member of cabin crew. If a serious event occurred then supplementary reports may be requested from all crew members.

Cabin defects log

Cabin Defects Log

Date:		Route:			
Flt No:		A/C Type:		A/C Reg:	
Captain:					
Purser/No1:					
Crew Member Reporting:				Crew No:	

Time		Defect	Rectified / Report	Signature
	1			
	2			
	3			
	4			
	5			

By signing below I confirm that I have carried out the required reporting procedures to the Purser/No1 to report defect 1 2 3 4 5 (circle as necessary)

Signature: _____   Print name: _____

Crew number: _____

Date: _____   Time: _____

The cabin defects log remains on board the aircraft. It is used to record any breakages, damage or use of emergency equipment. The log is completed on every flight with brief details of any issues, e.g. tray table for seat 10a has a broken hinge, the aisle carpet at the rear of the aircraft is badly stained or the portable oxygen bottle adjacent to crew station 1 has been used.

Once the cabin crew have completed the cabin defects log it must be passed to the Captain. If emergency equipment has been used, or is faulty, the Captain will transfer the information to the aircraft technical log.

When the aircraft lands back in the UK, aircraft engineers will check the defects log and complete any required maintenance.

> **Did you know?** If there are no defects to report, the flight details, etc. are still completed and the comment NIL DEFECTS is written on the page.

There are a number of other documents which are completed as required:

- **Port health card** – this needs to be completed by passengers travelling on a flight where a passenger or a number of passengers experienced symptoms of an infectious disease, e.g. rashes or severe stomach upsets.

- **Disruptive passenger report** – there may be an occasion where a passenger becomes physically aggressive, drunk or verbally abusive. If the situation deteriorates, and the passenger does not respond to requests issued by the cabin crew, further action may need to be taken. This report may be used in a court of law if the airline decides to prosecute.

- **Witness form** – should an incident occur on board it is essential to get independent witness statements. These statements may subsequently be used if the airline decides to prosecute and they may be used as evidence in court.

- **Accident and incident report** – although the accident and/or incident will be noted on the flight report, for purposes of adhering to health and safety guidelines as well as monitoring these occurrences, a supplementary report will need to be completed. This report contains more detail of the accident/incident and may be used to update procedures, highlight training needs or as evidence should a passenger claim compensation for an injury at a later date.

2.   The role of cabin crew in ensuring safety and security

Legislation related to aviation security

One aspect of the role of cabin crew is to ensure the security of the passengers on their aircraft. Therefore, it is important to have a general understanding of the legislation which is in place to support the procedures and practices that will become an everyday occurrence when you are working for an airline.

National Aviation Security Programme (Department for Transport)

The mission of the Department for Transport is to put security measures and procedures in place to protect the travelling public, staff employed in the transport industry and the transport facilities themselves. The Department for Transport wants the travelling public to

23

be confident in transport security, but they do not want to impose too many restrictions which could affect passenger journeys. The Aviation Security Programme covers a range of aspects related to airports, air travel and airlines and is constantly being reviewed and updated in response to incidents, reports, feedback and consultation.

The Aviation and Maritime Security Act 1990

This legislation relates to both air and sea travel, e.g. ports and airports, and provides the framework for security staff to detain or challenge someone who is acting suspiciously in, or around, an airport. For example, if a passenger makes a joke to check-in staff about there being a bomb in their luggage, there is a sequence of events and warnings that the staff will go through. The passenger could be searched, arrested and even prosecuted.

Activity ➡

Visit this webpage to find out what happened to someone who made a hoax bomb threat to delay a flight as she was running late.
www.dailymail.co.uk/news/article-357942/Bomb-scare-girl

The Anti-Terrorism Crime and Security Act 2001

This piece of legislation was put in place following the terrorist attacks in New York on 11 September 2001. The Act amended the Terrorism Act of 2000 to include more guidance and increase police powers when dealing with potential terrorists or events that could have an impact on national security. The legislation makes it easier for the security forces to freeze assets, monitor asylum and immigration, adjust and extend criminal law, revise powers for preventing crime, increase the control of pathogens and toxins, and to enable access and retention of communication data, e.g. computers, laptops and mobile phones.

Did you know? A pathogen is something that can cause a disease and in this situation it would be life threatening, e.g. anthrax.

Security measures

As cabin crew you will be issued with an airside ID (identity) card. This card will give you access to the airside areas of the airport, i.e. those beyond security, passport control and customs. To obtain an ID card you will have to provide a range of evidence and proof of activities for a minimum of 5 years. Cabin crew are subject to the same security checks as the passengers before each flight.

Once on board the aircraft, and before the passengers arrive, cabin crew complete a series of security checks. They are looking for anything which is unusual, e.g. broken seals on a food cart, and challenging anyone who does not have a visible ID card.

As the passengers board the aircraft cabin crew check the boarding cards, watching passenger behaviour and reactions. This helps them to identify anyone who is nervous, anxious or appears unwell. Once the passengers have boarded and the aircraft is positioning for take-off, the flight deck door will be locked and access to the flight deck will be restricted to personnel who know the door code.

During the flight the cabin crew remain vigilant, observing passenger behaviour as they deliver the cabin service. On long flights, or night flights where the service is not constant, the cabin crew are expected to make 20 minute checks on the passenger cabin and the toilets. Cabin crew will also react promptly to passenger call bells. This could be someone who has been taken ill or a situation occurring which has resulted in other passengers alerting the crew or it could be accidental. Cabin crew should always respond to the blue light and distinctive sound of the passenger call bell.

As the aircraft is on descent into the destination airport the cabin crew will secure all carts, sealing and locking them, make sure all cupboards and stowage areas are secure to prevent objects being hidden in them during the turnaround process. Once the aircraft has landed, and all passengers have disembarked, the cabin crew will walk through the cabin, opening the overhead luggage bins, visually checking the floor areas underneath the seats and the seat pockets to check that nothing has been left on board the aircraft. Often people put their books in the seat pocket, or leave a bag of tax-free goods in the overhead bin and the cabin crew will notify the handling agent so that the passenger will be able to reclaim their goods. In terms of security, items that could cause harm to the aircraft, crew or passengers may also have been left on board and the cabin crew must be able to recognise these and follow procedures. When the aircraft is on the ground other people can gain access – cabin crew should challenge anyone who does not have a visible airside pass.

Types of threat

As cabin crew you are made aware of the types of threat to the aviation industry and you will receive training on how to deal with these situations. They are not an everyday occurrence and you may never experience any problems, but if you do you need to know how to react. In the aviation industry the threats could include:

- Terrorism – this is where fear is used to make people co-operate. Violent acts are committed to create fear and instigate an awareness of a cause. These violent acts are often used to stimulate a response by a government or gain publicity for a cause, e.g. the 9/11 terrorist attack on the Twin Towers in New York.

- Sabotage – is about causing disruption to normal operations. It could be someone who has a grudge against a particular company and who wants to damage the reputation of the airline. Sabotage can also lead to loss of life in extreme circumstances.

- Hijack – is when a group, or an individual, takes control of the aircraft during the journey. This will be through force or threats and the hijacker will make demands, e.g. to land at a different destination or to highlight a particular situation. In October 2000, two Saudi nationals used this method to inform the world of alleged human rights abuses in their country.

- Bomb threat – information about a bomb either at the airport or on a flight is carefully assessed and given a rating – green, amber or red – and action related to the level of danger is taken.

There are other situations that may occur during a flight which will need to be dealt with promptly and efficiently by the crew. From the moment passengers board the aircraft, until their disembarkation, the cabin crew's professionalism and authority should instill confidence in passengers and ensure their compliance. Getting the balance between the warm, friendly welcome on board and the importance of getting passengers to watch the safety demonstration, do up their seatbelts and switch off mobile phones is a skill to be learned.

3. Maintaining passenger compliance

The safety demonstration

When people think about the role of cabin crew they immediately remember the safety demonstration. Many assume that it is easy to complete, but it is not that simple! Firstly, the aircraft will have started to move towards the runway, the surface may be uneven and the cabin crew will be standing in the aisle wating for the senior member of cabin crew to start the passenger announcement. Secondly, passengers may be frequent travellers, excited about their holiday, tired and disinterested – they may not be paying attention. Finally, as a cabin crew member you may not have checked your emergency demonstration equipment before you stood in your demonstration position.

How do you get their attention?

The senior cabin crew member will start the passenger announcment with a brief introduction. This gives the passengers time to 'tune in' while the cabin crew reinforce the importance of the message.

> **Did you know?** On some airlines the Captain will introduce himself/herself and the cabin crew while reminding passengers that they need to pay full attention to the safety demonstration.

Level 2 Introduction to Cabin Crew

Using communication techniques effectively encourages passengers to pay attention. The cabin crew position themselves in the cabin and place their demonstration equipment ready for use, thereby making passengers aware that something is about to happen. Placing the equipment in the sequence that it will be shown also ensures that it is ready for use, e.g. lifejacket tapes not tied, seat belt is extended and oxygen mask is not tangled.

The safety demonstration is always delivered before the aircraft takes off. Some airlines have a video which they show and other airlines use a manual demonstration. Whichever method is used it is vital that passengers give the cabin crew their full attention.

Did you know? In some aircraft evacuations, passengers have tried to use the exit that they used to board the aircraft rather than their nearest exit, which may have been behind them. In an explosive decompression, passengers only have seconds to put on an oxygen mask if they are going to survive.

Activity➡

Use YouTube to carry out some research on safety demonstrations on aircraft. Discuss the techniques used to gain passenger attention (Pegasus Airlines and Emirates use very different methods).

What do you think are the benefits of a manual (rather than video) safety demonstration?

Cabin secure checks

Once the safety demonstration has been completed the cabin crew complete cabin secure checks in preparation for take-off. Cabin secure checks involve:

- Making sure seatbelts are securely fastened
- Seat backs and seat tables are in the upright position
- Window blinds are open
- No hand luggage is obstructing exit routes
- Toilets are empty
- Galley equipment is secure

Once cabin crew have checked that the passenger cabin is ready for take-off, the flight deck will be informed and cabin crew take their seats and secure their seatbelts.

> **Did you know?** Cabin crew seats have a full inertia-reel harness with shoulder straps, whereas passengers have a lap strap. If a passenger has a baby on their lap they are given an extension to their seatbelt, which is attached to the adult one, and which provides the baby with their own lap strap. Passengers who need longer seatbelts are also given an extension to their lap strap to ensure that they are secure.

The cabin secure process is also completed before landing and is usually started when the aircraft has started to descend and the 'fasten seatbelt' sign comes on.

4.   Dealing with medical issues

People may become unwell on flights for a variety of reasons. Cabin crew are trained to recognise symptoms and provide first-aid where appropriate. The principles of first-aid are:

1.   Preserving life
2.   Preventing the condition from getting worse
3.   Promoting recovery

First-aid situations can range from a nose bleed to a heart attack, asthma to ear pain, miscarriage to vomiting. Cabin crew must be ready to respond; even as a new crew member, if you are the first to respond to the passenger you will need to assess the situation and be ready to take action.

> **Did you know?** The process of flying can often cause people to get stressed; they worry about not getting to the airport on time, will their luggage be over the allowed weight/size, have they remembered passports and tickets, will the aircraft crash. The fears that people have are personal, but they can sometimes have the effect of making people ill.

Some of the health problems can be minor medical issues, e.g. indigestion, fainting or a nose bleed, while others may be more serious, e.g. a heart attack, choking or asthma attacks. How cabin crew deal with the situation is important. The passengers expect that the cabin crew, through training and experience, will know what to do in such a situation and to remain calm and in control. If the medical situation is serious, the cabin crew may request the assistance of a medically-qualified person.

Remember, you are at 35,000 feet... how can you do this?

1. Do a PA (public address announcement) asking if there is a medically-qualified person on board the flight, e.g. a doctor, nurse or paramedic (they will need to provide evidence of their qualification).

2. Request ground-to-air assistance, e.g. from a company such as Medlink. A medically-trained person will ask for information about the passenger's condition, make a diagnosis and suggest appropriate treatment/action.

3. Divert to the nearest airport and arrange for an ambulance and medical staff to board the aircraft.

If a first-aid situation occurs, it is important that cabin crew respond quickly and appropriately. Staff are trained to never ignore a passenger call bell – it could be someone asking for another drink or it could be someone who is unwell and by ignoring it the situation may become more serious.

Actions by cabin crew

If the situation is minor then the attending cabin crew member will deal with it, taking time to talk to the passenger, finding out what the problem is and providing treatment. If appropriate, one cabin crew member will remain with the passenger and signal for another crew member to get any equipment or medication required.

> **Did you know?** A good cabin crew member is someone who is observant, responsive and quick to assess situations, e.g. if the call bell rings and another cabin crew member responds you will check to make sure that they do not need your support. Remember that cabin crew work as a team and support each other.

In medical situations the principle of **DR ABC** is followed by cabin crew:

1. The first person to arrive on the scene will assess the situation and the passenger (acting calmly, confidently and quickly). Ensure that there is no **dange**r to yourself or the passenger. Do not move the passenger unless absolutely necessary. Think about your personal safety, e.g. use protective gloves.

2. Check the passenger for a **response**. Can they hear you, do they respond to touch? If they can hear you tell them your name and reassure them, while finding out any information that may help you to assess the situation.

3. You need to make sure that the passenger's **airway** is unblocked. Check to make sure there is no blockage in the throat. To keep the airway clear, tilt the head back with the neck extended.

4. Is the passenger **breathing?** Look for breathing for 10 seconds, checking to see if the chest rises. Listen for the sound of breathing from the passenger's mouth or nose. Feel for the chest rise or put your cheek near to the passenger's mouth to feel for the exhaled air.

5. The final check is for **circulation.** Can you feel a pulse? The pulse will indicate that the heart is pumping.

> **Did you know?** Be careful how you take a pulse. The best location to use on an adult is the pulse in the neck just below the jaw line – the carotid pulse. You can also find a pulse in the wrist, the radial pulse, but you need to be careful that you do not have your thumb on the inside of the wrist because you will be feeling your own pulse. On a baby, the brachial pulse is found on the inside of the arm midway between the elbow and shoulder.

In some circumstances it may be necessary to give CPR (cardio pulmonary resuscitation) to a passenger. This can be given manually or by using AED (automated external defibrillation) equipment.

Activity➡

Use the following You Tube video to find out about manual CPR.

| You Tube GB | vinnie jones hard and fast hands only cpr |

Level 2 Introduction to Cabin Crew

There are a series of protocols (rules) which must be observed when using the AED and only certain personnel that can use it. During initial training, cabin crew have an opportunity to observe and learn about this piece of equipment. However, it only the senior crew member who would control and direct the operation of the AED. The Captain must also be informed if the AED is going to be used.

Other items related to first-aid are located on board the aircraft, including:

- First-aid kit – FAK

- Emergency first-aid kit – EFAK

- Emergency medical kit – EMK or doctor's box

- Oxygen bottles

Cabin crew are trained in the location and use of the equipment and are tested during their initial training programme, their annual SEP (Safety and Emergency Procedures) training, any promotion courses and before every flight. As part of the pre-flight briefing the senior cabin crew member will ask emergency, security and first-aid questions. This should be done in a supportive way, not to embarrass or make any crew member uncomfortable, but to ensure that each member of cabin crew is focused and ready for the flight.

> **Did you know?** Medical situations **do not** occur on every flight, but cabin crew must be prepared and know how to respond when they do. Time can be crucial in certain circumstances, while other situations may just need reassurance and a tablet.

From beginning to end a flight can be eventful. Although most flights are routine, cabin crew must never be complacent, should always be observant, confident and ready to take action

when necessary. Cabin crew are there to ensure passenger health and safety, as well as making sure that security standards are maintained and procedures are followed.

03 Aircraft emergency situations

Introduction

As we've seen so far, the main role of cabin crew is to ensure the safety of passengers and to do this you will be trained in various procedures and protocols (rules). Each airline delivers its own training programme to new cabin crew recruits. In all cases, the training is very structured and is constantly reviewed and checked by the CAA to ensure that airlines are maintaining industry standards.

Training for emergencies takes place during the first weeks of an initial cabin crew training programme and involves both theory and practical exercises. New recruits are required to achieve a minimum pass mark in order to continue with their training. There are no short cuts – you have to learn facts and demonstrate your understanding through written exams and practical activities. Some of the procedures are only completed during initial training, for example the aircraft ditching simulation. Cabin crew may need to update procedures, for example flight crew incapacitation, if different aircraft types are purchased by the company.

Every year cabin crew take their SEP (Safety and Emergency Procedures) exams. They may also receive training on new procedures and industry updates.

This unit will help you to develop your knowledge and understanding of:

- Aircraft emergency situations
- How to respond using correct procedures
- The type of equipment available on board the aircraft
- The principles of survival following an aircraft emergency
- The practical skills necessary to demonstrate procedures e.g. aircraft emergency evacuation

Level 2 Introduction to Cabin Crew

Learning Outcomes	Assessment Criteria
1 Understand how to respond to aircraft emergencies	**1.1** Define the terms planned and unplanned emergencies **1.2** Identify flight crew instructions for planned emergency landing/ditching **1.3** Explain procedures for preparing and evacuating the cabin for a planned emergency including: - Landing - Ditching **1.4** Explain how to deal with an unplanned emergency **1.5** Identify the type of passengers not suitable to be able bodied passengers **1.6** Describe the different types of brace position and their purpose **1.7** Identify positive commands which should be used during evacuation **1.8** Outline techniques for maintaining crowd control **1.9** Identify factors which can prevent an aircraft exit from being used in an evacuation **1.10** State the occasions when cabin crew must initiate an evacuation without the flight crew's command **1.11** Explain what to do if an aircraft exit is unserviceable and cannot be used in an emergency
2 Know on board emergency procedures	**2.1** Describe aircraft emergency equipment including location **2.2** Describe emergency situations that could occur on board an aircraft **2.3** State the elements which must be present to sustain a fire **2.4** Identify types of fire extinguisher and the types of fire they are suitable for fighting **2.5** Describe the purpose and basic principles of a smoke hood **2.6** Describe the role of cabin crew on board in fighting fires **2.7** Identify how to recognise the signs of slow decompression **2.8** Identify how to recognise the signs of rapid decompression **2.9** Describe the crew responsibilities following a decompression **2.10** Identify how to recognise light, moderate and severe turbulence

Level 2 Introduction to Cabin Crew

	2.11 Describe the actions to be taken for different levels of turbulence 2.12 Explain the main actions taken by the cabin crew during a flight crew incapacitation drill
3 Be able to follow on board emergency procedures	3.1 Operate fire extinguishers on board 3.2 Operate a smoke hood 3.3 Evacuate an aircraft in a planned emergency
4 Know the primary principles for survival after an airline emergency	4.1 State the main principles of survival 4.2 Describe techniques for survival at sea 4.3 Describe techniques for survival in: - arctic conditions - the desert - the jungle

1. Understand how to respond to aircraft emergencies

Aircraft emergencies are either planned or unplanned.

A *planned* emergency is when the captain has time to inform the cabin crew and they have time to prepare. An *unplanned* emergency occurs with no warning and cabin crew must rely on their initiative and responses developed through their knowledge and training.

An unplanned emergency is more likely to occur during take-off or landing, e.g. a fire in an engine on take-off will require the pilot to terminate the procedure and is similar to an emergency stop in a car. The pilots must then carry out a series of actions to complete the abandoned take-off and maintain control of the aircraft. This may result in a time delay before being able to inform the cabin crew of exactly what is happening. This is the reason why cabin crew are trained to go through a period of silent review when they are seated in their crew positions on their jump seats for take-off and landing.

> **Did you know?** The idea of silent review is to have a heightened awareness of the aircraft performance (noise and movement), an opportunity to observe passengers for any anxiety or distress and, most importantly, for each crew member to focus on the main functions of their job – safety, security and the welfare of passengers.

35

In a planned emergency the Captain will have had prior warning of the situation and will inform the cabin crew of the actions they need to take. The cabin crew are alerted to the situation by either a call on the cabin interphone or a coded message on the PA (public address system).

Did you know? Phones are located at crew stations throughout the aircraft and are used for communicating with other cabin crew members, i.e. No. 1 in the front galley checking with No. 2 in the rear galley that all meals are cooked and ready for service.

The interphone can also be used to deliver public address (PA) announcements to the passengers, e.g. if the aircraft is experiencing turbulence and the fasten seatbelt sign is put on, the No. 1 will inform passengers to remain seated and do up their seatbelt.

The interphone can also be used by the flight deck (pilots) to contact cabin crew either through an alert signal (the phone chimes have a different tone in an emergency) or by calling in the normal way.

Once the cabin crew have been alerted to the situation, by either a call on the cabin interphone or a coded message on the public address system, they must react accordingly and the training they have received will be put into practice. They are trained to be calm and in control. If they were serving meals, they will return the carts to the galley (kitchen) areas and put them back in their stowage. The senior cabin crew member collects their EPB (Emergency Procedures Booklet) from their crew position and goes to the flight deck for an information exchange. The back page of the booklet is usually used to make notes – NITS.

Did you know? The mnemonic NITS means:

N = Nature of the emergency
I = Intention, e.g. what action the Captain will be taking
T = Time, e.g. how much time until landing
S = Special instructions, e.g. evacuate using left side only

Once the senior member of cabin crew (often called the Purser/No.1) has collected all of the information and recorded it onto the NITS page, having checked and confirmed details with the Captain, they will return to the cabin and share the information with the rest of the cabin crew, who will also note the details down on the NITS page of their own EPB booklets. Watches will be synchronised (the Purser/No.1 will already have checked the time on their watch with the flight crew to make sure it matches) – this is done to ensure that the aircraft crew are all working within the same time frame and will be ready for the landing.

Preparation for a planned landing

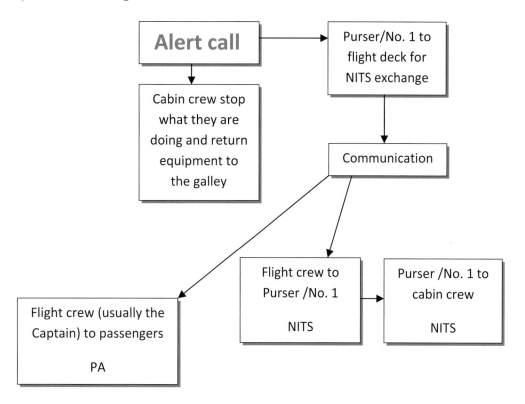

It is now time to prepare the passengers and the cabin for landing as follows:

- Passenger briefing
- Preparing passengers
- Securing the cabin
- Preparing self
- Collecting useful equipment
- Selecting ABPs (able-bodied passengers)

How much preparation is completed will depend on the time until impact.

Did you know? Each emergency situation is different and the time until landing and types of situation will determine how much preparation can be completed. The selection of equipment to be used is also be affected by the type of emergency, e.g. are you landing on water or on land?

Activity ➡

Use the internet to research air crash investigations and reconstructions.

You Tube ᴳᴮ ≡ ▾ | air crash investigation | 🔍

Preparing the passengers focuses on giving them advice and guidance to increase their chances of survival. One major aspect of the crash landing is getting passengers into the 'brace' position.

ASSUME BRACE POSITION

Activity ➡

Try out the 'brace' position sitting in your chair. How would it protect you in an emergency impact? For example, which parts of your body are you protecting?

The CAA (Civil Aviation Authority) investigates air accidents and changes to procedures may be implemented following their findings, e.g. the Kegworth air disaster in 1989 resulted in changes to the brace position.

Selecting and briefing ABPs (able-bodied passengers) is another aspect of preparation that is designed to improve survival rates during an aircraft evacuation. In an emergency landing, a speedy evacuation is vital, since there may be a risk of fire – within 90 seconds fire can penetrate the external shell of the fuselage especially if it is intense. In a ditching situation, a controlled landing onto water, speed is not as important providing the aircraft is intact and water is not rushing into the cabin.

Level 2 Introduction to Cabin Crew

> **Did you know?** The fuselage is the cylindrical main body section of the aircraft. The passenger cabin, the flight deck and the hold are all located in this section.

ABPs are selected and briefed to supplement the cabin crew role. They can help to:

- Hold back passengers to prevent people jumping out before the evacuation slides are fully inflated
- Assist in opening exits
- Assist at the bottom of the evacuation slides to get passengers up and away to prevent congestion
- In exceptional circumstances, take over if cabin crew are incapacitated

Certain passengers would **not** be suitable as ABPs; the mnemonic PINCODE is used to help identify these categories:

Pregnant (on certain flights it could also stand for prisoner)
Intoxicated (could also be people who are ill or infirm)
Nervous
Child (also think carefully about passengers with young children)
Obese
Disabled (could also stand for deportees)
Elderly

When the preparations have been completed, the senior member of cabin crew confirms to the flight crew that "*the cabin is ready*" for the emergency landing and that "*preparations have been completed*".

The cabin crew will be told from the flight deck "*cabin crew seats for landing*" – this is the signal for the crew to be at their designated crew seats, fastening their seatbelts and preparing to get into their brace positions.

> **Did you know?** The cabin crew brace positions are different from those of the passengers. The cabin crew seats have a full harness with straps that go over their shoulders and fit into the lap buckle. The harness has an inertia action (similar to that of a car seatbelt). Cabin crew seats face either the back or the front of the aircraft and the brace position is adapted to minimise the whiplash effect.

At a signal (usually a command over the PA) cabin crew will, from their brace position, shout out "*brace, brace, stay down, stay low*". They should shout in turn (there are usually 2 crew members at each exit route) to keep the instructions clear and audible. The cabin crew will keep the momentum going to make sure passengers stay down and protect themselves until the aircraft has come to a final stop.

> **Did you know?** There is likely to be more than one impact… think of a pebble skimming on water or dropping an object onto the ground.

Once the aircraft has come to a complete stop, the announcement "*attention, cabin crew to stations*" alerts the cabin crew to go to their exits and check for any fire, hazard or obstruction. The flight crew complete the engine shutdown procedure and then give the command "*evacuate, evacuate*".

The cabin crew, assisted by the ABPs, open the exits and evacuate the passengers. To make sure that passengers know what to do, cabin crew shout instructions such as "*undo your seatbelts, come this way, no hand luggage*".

These instructions need to be delivered in an assertive manner, using short and positive statements, with plenty of repetition. Remember – there will be a lot of background noise, people will be panicking, they may be hurt and there may be a lot of external noise, e.g. fire engine sirens.

> **Did you know?** Once the passengers start to move, they will follow each other and the cabin crew need to ensure that the flow is constant. Using arm gestures, members of cabin crew stand so that they can be seen and keep encouraging passengers to come towards the exit. Once the flow is established and the passengers reach the door exit, the commands change. Remember the CAA requirement is to evacuate an aircraft in 90 seconds.

When passengers get to the door and the escape slide, the cabin crew change the instructions and tell them how to go down the slide, "*jump , jump, jump and sit, keep moving, stay close together*".

The evacuation process is different in a ditching situation, so different instructions are given. There is no need to jump onto the slide, which has now become a raft floating at the level of the door sill. Instead, passengers are told to step into or crawl onto the slide. In some instances the passengers might need to get into the water and then climb into the slide raft.

Not every situation is straightforward and it is impossible to give specific instructions to cover every eventuality. Cabin crew are given guidelines in their training, but on some occasions they will need to use their own initiative, for example:

- External hazards preventing an exit door from opening, e.g. fire, debris, buildings, trees, etc.
- Operational problems, e.g. the evacuation slide not inflating, door jammed, etc.
- Communication breakdown, e.g. flight crew dead or unconscious on impact
- Structural damage to aircraft, e.g. breaking into 3 pieces on impact
- Landing position, e.g. upside down, sideward or on a steep incline
- Weather, e.g. strong winds affecting evacuation slides

All of these situations have occurred and people have survived.

In the instance of landing on water – a ditching – the majority of the procedure is the same in terms of cabin preparation. The main differences occur when passengers are instructed to put on their lifejackets and, during the evacuation process, when they may be using the slide as a life raft.

Remember – in an unplanned emergency, there is little time to prepare the passengers and communication may be limited. Cabin crew must rely on the training they receive on their initial programme, plus their annual SEP (Safety and Emergency Procedures) course and examination to ensure that their reactions are appropriate and prompt.

> **Did you know?** After any incident, procedures and actions are reviewed and modifications made be made, for example saying "*stay down, stay low*" as an instruction for the brace position is often more effective than shouting "*brace, brace*", which passengers may interpret as an instruction to sit upright with arms rigid against the seat in front of them.

2.   Knowing on-board emergency procedures

Emergency landings are only one of safety procedures that cabin crew are expected to know about. There are a variety of other situations and procedures which individuals need to be familiar with, including:

- Fire
- Decompression
- Turbulence
- Pilot incapacitation
- Medical
- Hijack

Cabin crew also need to be familiar with how to use emergency equipment, where to find it, any restrictions that need to be considered when using it and how long it lasts for.

> **Did you know?** The oxygen supply to a smoke hood lasts for 15 minutes, but if the crew member wearing it is breathing rapidly and deeply it may mean that the supply does not last that long.

Fire

For any fire to occur 3 factors are required, making up the so-called 'fire triangle':

- Fuel – any substance, whether a solid, liquid or gas, which will burn

- Oxygen – this is supplied by the surrounding air

- Heat – this could be something which is already burning or an electrical short circuit

> **Did you know?** Sources of ignition can be:
>
> 1. Flames – once a flammable atmosphere is present a fire will quickly spread
> 2. Sparks – produced by electrical wiring or friction
> 3. Hot surfaces – these may ignite a flammable atmosphere if the surface temperature exceeds the ignition temperature of the fuel source, e.g. grease in an oven

The basic principle of extinguishing a fire is to remove one or more of the 3 factors:

1. Starve – remove or limit the fuel, e.g. switch off electrics
2. Smother – starve or dilute the oxygen content, e.g. use a fire extinguisher
3. Cool – remove heat, e.g. use water or water-based liquids to lower the temperature

Level 2 Introduction to Cabin Crew

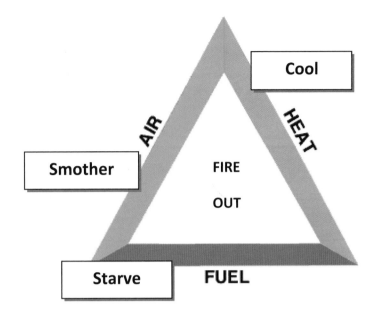

The danger from an internal fire during a flight can be catastrophic. Prompt action and firefighting training is absolutely essential. To deal with a fire, the cabin crew must work as a team. Firefighting can be made more difficult by the cramped conditions and the presence of frightened passengers.

Did you know? The aircraft may take 20 minutes to get to the ground from a cruising altitude. Therefore, all types of cabin fire must be treated with the same degree of urgency.

Decompression

During the cruise phase of a flight the aircraft could be at 33,000–39,000 feet above sea level. At these heights it is impossible to survive due to a lack of oxygen in the outside atmosphere and the extreme cold. Inside the aircraft is a controlled environment – the cabin altitude is kept lower than the height at which the aircraft is actually flying. Cabin pressure is maintaining an internal cabin altitude of between 6,000–8,000 feet by compressing the cabin air to a similar pressure to that at sea level. The pressurised air is fed into the cabin from the aircraft engines.

Any loss of cabin pressure is known as 'decompression'. The internal cabin altitude starts to increase to that of the actual flight altitude, oxygen supplies reduce and hypoxia can occur.

Did you know? Hypoxia is a shortage of oxygen to the body blood cells. The brain becomes quickly affected and although people think they are acting normally their muscle co-ordination deteriorates, severe trembling occurs, eyesight becomes affected, fingertips become blue and the face grey. If oxygen is not made available people will go into a coma and die.

43

There are 2 types of decompression:

- Explosive or rapid decompression – caused by a fracture in the fuselage or an explosion
- Slow decompression – caused by a slight engine malfunction, a faulty door seal or a minor crack in a window seal

> **Did you know?** Imagine shaking a can of drink and then opening it, if you do it slowly you may be able to stop the can contents going over you , if you do it quickly then the contents go everywhere (rapid decompression).

The signs for each type of decompression are different:

With *rapid decompression* (a sudden loss of cabin pressure), there will be a loud explosive noise, mist vapour in the cabin, the aircraft will go into a steep dive, the oxygen masks will drop down, carbonated drinks explode and hot liquids boil. The passengers and cabin crew will need to breathe rapidly, while ears and sinuses will be painful. Any loose items in the cabin will be drawn out of any 'hole' in the fuselage. There will be changes in the noise level and severe vibration of the aircraft.

If *slow decompression* (a gradual loss of cabin pressure) occurs, ears will pop, passengers and cabin crew may feel dizzy or light-headed, tired and possibly nauseous. There may be a whistling noise close to the area of the gradual leak, for example at a door where the door seal has become slightly damaged. The instruments in the flight deck will show a gradual loss of cabin pressure. This loss of pressure can be managed and the aircraft can continue the flight. The Captain would inform the airline engineers and the aircraft would be scheduled for maintenance.

In the case of a rapid decompression it is essential that everybody grabs an oxygen mask and secures themselves in a seat until the aircraft has reached a safe altitude where oxygen is not required, i.e. below 10,000 feet. In the passenger cabin there is an oxygen mask for each seated passenger and there are extra masks located throughout the cabin for infants seated on their parent's lap, in the toilets and galley areas as well as at crew stations.

Turbulence

Anyone who has been on a flight will have experienced some form of turbulence. It is caused by a number of conditions, usually related to weather, but also a range of other situations affecting air flow, such as:

- Thermals
- The jet stream
- Mountains
- Wake turbulence
- Micro bursts

Activity ➡

Use the internet to help you research and give a brief definition for each of the terms used above. Can you explain why this condition might affect aircraft?

Light turbulence is similar to travelling on a slightly bumpy road and does not usually last very long. It would not be necessary for the cabin service to be stopped and people can still walk around the aircraft.

Moderate turbulence is more intense and usually lasts for 10-15 minutes, although it may last longer, and there will be breaks in between. Passengers have the sensation of the aircraft going up and down, similar to a gentle theme park ride. Walking is difficult and cabin service will be stopped. The fasten seatbelt sign will be activated and cabin crew secure all loose items and complete a cabin secure check.

Severe turbulence is more of a white-knuckle ride and the aircraft can drop dramatically. This situation is very unusual and can result in injuries to passengers and crew if immediate action is not taken.

Passengers are advised to have their seatbelts loosely fastened at all times during the flight. For take-off and landing the seatbelt needs to be tight, but during the cruise section of the flight it can be looser, but if any turbulence occurs it can quickly be tightened to help prevent injury.

Pilot incapacitation

If a pilot becomes ill during the flight, the pilot in control of the aircraft, either the Captain or the First Officer depending on who has been taken ill, will call the senior member of cabin crew to the flight deck. The call could be an announcement over the PA using coded words or an alert call on the cabin interphone. The cabin crew member nearest to the flight deck will also attend.

Did you know? The controls on either side of the flight deck are exactly the same, which means that the pilot flying the aircraft has control of the instruments. The system is similar to the dual controls in a driving school car, which enables your instructor to take over if necessary. But it does mean that if one pilot becomes unconscious and falls onto the controls it can affect the aircraft stability.

On arriving in the flight deck the cabin crew may need to move the 'unconscious' pilot away from the controls to ensure that the remaining pilot can proceed with the flight and land the aircraft safely. Each situation is different and actions may need to be modified once the pilot incapacitation drill has been completed – the immediate priority is to get the incapacitated pilot away from the controls.

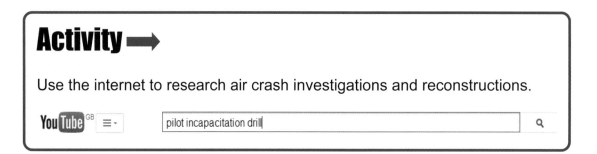

3. Following on-board emergency procedures

The previous section of this unit has explained in detail the range and variety of on-board emergency procedures that members of cabin crew must be trained to address in an efficient and effective way.

Being able to *follow* emergency procedures is also very important – it's not enough just to know what they are! This includes being able to operate firefighting equipment and evacuate an aircraft in a planned emergency. There is equipment on board every aircraft to assist with firefighting and, as part of their training, cabin crew have the opportunity to use fire extinguishers to control fires. They also experience what it is like to wear a smoke hood and

Level 2 Introduction to Cabin Crew

complete search and rescue activities in a smoke-filled environment. Their training also includes practical sessions on aircraft evacuation techniques.

> **Did you know?** In the cabin, an individual not wearing PBE (protective breathing equipment), such as a smoke hood, is likely to be overcome by toxic smoke and fumes within 15-20 seconds. The PBE also protects the wearer from flames and heat which can cause damage to eyes and skin.

An important aspect of the role of cabin crew is being vigilant at all times, being aware of warning signs, being able to identify the types and sources of fire, collecting the appropriate firefighting equipment and fighting the fire.

4. Primary principles for survival after an airline emergency

Not all aircraft emergency landings take place at an airport with emergency services ready to rescue passengers. Some emergency landings have occurred in fairly deserted, inhospitable areas and survival has been a major challenge. One example is the 1972 Andes air crash, when an aircraft crash landed in mountains in South America on 13 October 1972 and survivors were not rescued until 23 December that year.

Airline communication systems used in emergencies are now much more sophisticated. SAR (search and rescue) procedures are more quickly deployed and international agreements covering most of the world's land and sea areas ensure co-operation and support to locate and rescue survivors. Therefore, the most important priority is to *survive,* which means staying alive until rescued.

There are four principles of survival:

1. Protection – protection from the environment, whether hot or cold, wet or dry, but also protection from injury or disease

2. Location – systems are in place to notify search and rescue (SAR) of aircraft location, but sometimes these will need to be re-enforced to pinpoint the location of survivors

3. Water – the body can survive for at least 2 days without water and, in some situations, people have been known to survive for 11 days

4. Food – although difficult to believe, people can survive up to 3 weeks without food

Level 2 Introduction to Cabin Crew

> **Did you know?** Because of the wide range of air routes worldwide, an emergency landing could take place in the sea, the jungle, a desert or in Arctic conditions. To survive, passengers and crew must adapt and prioritise, remembering that the most important aspect is protection and the least important is food.

During initial training to become air cabin crew the emergency procedures section is very intense and you will need to learn and memorise procedures and drills. On an annual basis you will be tested on your knowledge and every time you fly you will be asked an emergency question. On every flight you will check certain pieces of emergency equipment. Changes may be made to procedures and you will update your knowledge through company notices and experiences. You will have the support of colleagues and systems in place to help you, but you also need to be focused, interested and realise that you never stop learning while working as cabin crew.

04 Dealing with passengers on board an aircraft

Introduction

As a member of cabin crew you will be expected to deliver excellent customer service at all times. Every passenger likes to be treated as an individual and cabin crew must respond to their needs. There are sometimes constraints that may have an impact on service delivery, for example a short flight time, safety issues and a limited range of products on board, but the way in which you deal with them will decide whether the customer leaves your flight with a positive impression of you and the airline.

Excellent customer service is at the heart of every airline's operations and cabin crew must work together to serve their passengers with the highest standards of customer care in line with company policies and in relation to health, safety and security.

This unit will help you to develop your knowledge and understanding of:

- Dealing with passengers who have special requirements
- How to provide effective customer service
- Dealing with passenger problems and complaints
- Working as part of a team
- How to handle conflict and incidents

Level 2 Introduction to Cabin Crew

Learning Outcomes	Assessment Criteria
1 Know how to deal with passengers who have special requirements	**1.1** Identify different types of airline passengers **1.2** Identify the range of passenger needs **1.3** Explain how to brief a blind passenger **1.4** Identify on-board requirements for guide dogs **1.5** Explain how to brief a deaf passenger **1.6** Identify the requirements for the carriage of pregnant passengers **1.7** Identify on-board considerations for unaccompanied minors **1.8** Identify the requirements for Passengers with Reduced Mobility (PRMs) **1.9** Identify relevant passenger codes
2 Understand how to provide effective customer service	**2.1** Identify the purpose of customer service **2.2** Describe the range of interpersonal skills required for effective customer service **2.3** Explain how customer service affects the success of the airline
3 Know how to deal with passenger problems and complaints	**3.1** Identify common causes of passenger problems and complaints **3.2** Outline ways of dealing with passenger problems and complaints **3.3** Identify different methods of communication when dealing with passenger problems and complaints **3.4** Describe how personal presentation, approach and attitude will influence the behaviour of the passenger
4 Know how to work as part of a team	**4.1** Identify the skills required for effective team working **4.2** Describe how to maintain effective working relationships
5 Know how to handle incidents and conflict situations	**5.1** Identify the chain of command when managing passenger conflicts **5.2** Describe the importance of co-ordination and co-operation between the crew **5.3** Identify types of incidents and conflict situations that could occur on board an aircraft **5.4** Describe how different personality types face conflict situations

6 Be able to deal with passengers	**6.1** Deal with conflict situations with passengers **6.2** Adapt methods of communication and behaviour to meet the individual needs of passengers

1.   Passengers with special requirements

It is important to understand that 'special requirements' are not limited to passengers with a disability. The nature of the airline industry is diverse – there are companies that operate charter flights, those that operate scheduled flights and some companies that offer both options.

Did you know? A charter flight is one where a tour operator contracts an aircraft for a given period of time, e.g. to provide flights for package holidays to Mediterranean destinations over a summer season. A scheduled flight is one that operates to a timetable and offers seat-only sales.

The many types of passengers using airlines often have very different needs, for example:

- A business traveller on a flight to New York may require a power supply for their laptop and a seat that converts into a bed
- Someone on a leisure flight will appreciate an entertainment system
- A family on a package holiday will want seats together
- An elderly person may need extra time or help to board the aircraft
- A passenger may have particular dietary needs, e.g. a gluten-free meal
- A person with restricted mobility may need physical help to get them to their seat
- A pregnant woman may need an extension seatbelt
- A child travelling on their own will need more individual attention than one travelling with a family

Level 2 Introduction to Cabin Crew

There are many other categories of passengers who can manage in their normal everyday environment, but whose needs may change while on an aircraft. The space on the aircraft is restricted, access points are not at ground level and passengers need to be aware of what could happen in an emergency.

A passenger with a visual impairment will be pre-boarded onto the aircraft, meaning that they are brought out to the aircraft before the other passengers. The cabin crew will already be aware of the passenger through the notification system that airlines use to inform cabin crew of PRMs (passengers with reduced mobility). One member of the cabin crew, usually the senior crew member of the section the passenger is seated in, will introduce themselves, put the passenger at their ease and then explain that they would like to familiarise them with the exit route and the safety demonstration.

Did you know? Often when sighted people are helping visually-impaired or blind people they forget that this person cannot see the actions that are being made. For example, instead of just reaching out to take the person's arm you need to tell them what you are going to do. When you want to take that passenger to the exit do not grab their arm and propel them to the exit, but allow them to take your arm, let them count how many rows to the exit, feel around the door frame and answer any questions they may have.

Activity →

Experience how it feels to be guided when you cannot see where you are going. Working in pairs, one person should to wear a blindfold that obscures their vision while the other person leads them around obstacles to a doorway. Now change roles and discuss how you felt.

How are you going to communicate effectively with a deaf passenger or someone whose first language is not English? In these situations the communication emphasis must be visual and cabin crew need to ensure they have the passenger's attention for the safety demonstration. How crew deal with the situation requires empathy and flexibility.

Remember that there is very little privacy in the confined space of an aircraft and as cabin crew you need to ensure that you treat everyone equally according to their needs. During the pre-flight cabin crew briefing, information about special requirements will be shared and cabin crew will be allocated duties and responsibilities. For example, the No. 2 cabin crew member who has responsibility for checking the catering in the rear galley will be tasked with ensuring that any requested diabetic and kosher meals are on board.

Level 2 Introduction to Cabin Crew

> **Did you know?** Some types of meals are requested for medical reasons, e.g. a diabetic meal (DBML) and others may be for religious reasons, e.g. a Muslim meal (MOML). Passengers also have the choice to express their personal preference, for example by ordering a vegetarian meal (AVML).

The aviation industry uses codes to abbreviate information and it is useful to learn these. Some can be decoded easily, e.g. INF is an infant (a child under 2 years), while others may be more obscure, e.g. BBML a meal for an infant.

Activity ➡

Carry out some research on the internet about IATA codes. Produce your own list for different passenger types and meal options.

2. Providing effective customer service

As cabin crew you need to ensure that the customer service you deliver is of the highest standard; customer service is not only about how you deal with one situation, but also about how you are perceived, how you present yourself, how you interact with your colleagues, how you communicate with every person you meet and how you feel about yourself.

Delivering effective customer service is vital for the success of a business. Remember that passengers judge an airline on the experience they have had. From the moment you put on your uniform and report for work, you become part of that experience. Sometimes as cabin

Level 2 Introduction to Cabin Crew

crew you may have to compensate for poor customer service received at an earlier stage of the passenger's journey, perhaps a problem at airport check-in for example.

Wearing a uniform makes you visible to all passengers. Therefore, it is important that the uniform is worn correctly to the company standards. On the initial training course, new recruits are issued with their uniform and throughout the programme their appearance is monitored. The airline will also give advice on grooming and personal hygiene; working in a confined area can be unpleasant if someone has hygiene issues.

Did you know? Female cabin crew with long hair need to have it tied back; some airlines stipulate that it must be in a bun. For crew members with short hair, the style must not fall over the face and their hair colour should be 'natural'. The style you have must be easy to maintain and not require constant attention.

Communication with the passengers is another opportunity to create a good impression. A genuine smile and a friendly greeting to welcome the passenger on board is the first interaction they will have with the cabin crew.

One passenger reaction to a cheery good morning at 04.00 may be "*is it?*", but the remaining 150+ people on board may feel pleased and reassured that the crew are pleasant, awake and enthusiastic.

If passengers have a problem they may approach the cabin crew for a solution. Often problems can be resolved by the cabin crew being observant and dealing with the concern before it becomes an issue, e.g. a passenger sitting in the wrong seat. To prevent the situation from escalating, cabin crew can intervene in a pleasant manner and give an explanation of how the seat numbering works. It may be that the passenger does not want to sit on the inside seat because they need to visit the toilet frequently, so it is always important to listen to the passenger and sometimes negotiate.

How you as cabin crew deal with situations is important. You should always:

- Listen
- Stay calm
- Be assertive
- Consider the needs of the passenger
- Empathise
- Work as part of a team

Remember that everyone is an individual with their particular needs. Airlines set their own standards of customer service and part of the cabin crew selection process assesses the applicant's customer service delivery. New and existing staff receive training to develop skills and their performance is monitored via feedback from flight reports, customer comments and on-board observations.

3.   Dealing with passenger problems and complaints

There are many different types and levels of complaint, as well as different reasons for complaining. When a passenger complains about a lack of legroom, it may be because they are tired, claustrophobic, nervous or seeking special treatment. Of course they could be tall and find the seat that they have been allocated does not give them enough space to sit comfortably. Whatever the reason, the cabin crew should deal with the situation in a positive way taking time to find out what the underlying concern is. The solution offered will depend on the availability of empty seats on the aircraft, a situation which does not often occur on a charter or low-cost flight. It may be that the cabin crew advise the passenger to pre-book a seat for their return flight. For the current flight, the cabin crew may approach other passengers to find out if someone is prepared to move. If this is the case, the cabin crew may offer them a complimentary drink for their help.

How members of cabin crew deal with any on-board situation impacts on the company's reputation. Therefore, airlines ensure that all their cabin crew are familiar with their procedures and continually monitor situations via flight reports and customer feedback. Regular training and individual action plans are implemented to develop skills. Examples of good practice by cabin crew may be used throughout the company and individual members of staff may be rewarded by being selected to operate special flights, e.g. transporting the England football team to their match destination.

4.   How to work as part of a team

When a group of people come together to work towards a common goal they become a team. As a member of cabin crew, you may be working with colleagues you have never met

Level 2 Introduction to Cabin Crew

before, so how can you ensure that you operate as team? If the common goal is a successful flight with a high level of customer satisfaction, how can you achieve this?

One important aspect in establishing an effective team is the pre-flight briefing, when the cabin crew get together before going out to the aircraft. The briefing is structured and is led by the senior crew member who will establish their own position as the team leader. They will also find out about the skills that individual members of their team have, e.g. nursing experience, another language or an interest in a sales promotion. Throughout the process the senior member of cabin crew will be assessing crew members and encouraging interaction, helping all crew members to bond and to be comfortable with their colleagues.

For junior cabin crew, the pre-flight briefing is an opportunity for them to identify the chain of command and to realise that they can refer to more experienced colleagues if there is something they are not confident with. For senior staff, they will be able to identify how they can give support and ensure that the flight is a success. Often new staff bring new ideas and they may have more recent knowledge if they have just completed their training course. They may also be nervous and they need to know that they are a valued team member.

Did you know? A good team leader is not somebody who terrifies other members of staff. They should not *demand* respect because they have been given the title of leader, but they must *gain* respect by treating each individual fairly, while being supportive and constructive.

The senior member of cabin crew sets goals and objectives during the pre-flight briefing. They communicate these to the team and make sure that everyone has an understanding of the requirements and how to achieve them. This may be the only time the whole crew is together in one place until the post-flight briefing, so it is vital that a good working relationship is established. It is also an opportunity to develop trust and mutual accountability.

© 2015 Travel & Tourism Publishing Ltd

Level 2 Introduction to Cabin Crew

Once on the aircraft, the cabin crew operate in their designated crew position and each position has specific duties to perform. It is important that each cabin crew member feels empowered to take action, but also that they can rely on each other when support is necessary, e.g. if a fire occurs on board and the most junior crew member is the first on the scene they must take action and not wait for the more senior person to take control.

Team dynamics change and cabin crew must be adaptable at all times. For example, using your initiative and dealing with an anxious passenger may mean that other members of the crew have to perform your duties, but it may also mean that a more serious situation does not develop, e.g. someone trying to open the aircraft door. However, team members need to be considerate of their colleagues and if you are always sitting and talking to passengers, while leaving your colleagues to get on with the meal service, you may be challenged about your career choice.

Teamwork is about good communication, being responsive and supporting each other. Identify your strengths, be aware of others' strengths and have respect (not just for people who have been cabin crew for a long time, but also for the newest member of the team). In emergency situations, you will rely on each other so mutual respect, communication and sharing ideas are some of the life skills that must be developed.

> **Discussion Point ⟷**
>
> *"Remember that there is no 'I' in team"* is a phrase often heard in industry. Discuss with a partner what this means and the importance of this phrase to members of cabin crew.

During initial training, cabin crew are trained on cabin service procedures and are made aware of the importance of the interactions they have with customers. Each airline has its own vision and mission statement, and you must recognise the responsibility you have as an individual to deliver and develop the company's reputation. You could be part of the team that changes someone's opinions about an airline – make sure it is a positive one.

5.   Handling incidents and conflict situations

Incidents are events that can occur on board an aircraft. These could be:

- Medical – these include situations where the reaction of the cabin crew is observed by passengers who are not directly involved with the incident. When dealing with a medical incident the cabin crew need to be aware of the proximity of other passengers and the nature of the illness. What happens if a passenger has a heart attack? As cabin crew you would all work as a team, utilising the individual skills each person brings to the situation. A confident, positive approach will reassure not only the passenger who is unwell, but their companions and other passengers on the flight.

Level 2 Introduction to Cabin Crew

- Spillages – these can occur when serving passengers their meal or drinks. The spillage could be the result of slight turbulence or someone pushing past. The correct procedure is to apologise, immediately take action to minimise the damage, get the attention of another crew member to assist and obtain the passenger's name and address so that their contact details can be logged on the flight report with an overview of the incident.

- Disregard of instructions – if a passenger disrupts the safety demonstration, perhaps because they are a frequent flyer and know what to do, the cabin crew member in that section should quietly speak to them and remind them that, for some passengers, this may be their first aircraft flight.

These are just a few of the events that can occur on a flight. If they are dealt with in a professional manner, using appropriate words and body language, they are usually easily resolved.

Conflict occurs when an issue has developed into an argument and there are factors which can escalate this type of situation, including:

- Alcohol – people can become drunk more quickly on board an aircraft due to the effects of altitude on the body. Some passengers who are anxious about flying may start drinking before they board the aircraft and continue once on board. If cabin crew notice a passenger, or group of passengers, becoming drunk they would politely inform them that they will not be served any more alcohol. The approach that the cabin crew use and the nature of the passenger(s) can affect the outcome; some people who drink a lot may then fall asleep, some people become aggressive and demanding, while others may not argue at all, but then start to drink alcohol they purchased in the tax-free shop before boarding the aircraft.

> **Did you know?** It is illegal to board an aircraft drunk and passengers can be prevented from getting on a flight. Cabin crew have the right to refuse to sell alcohol, the right to control the amount of alcohol consumed and the right to remove alcohol from a passenger.

- Drugs – as with alcohol, some people use non-prescribed drugs to 'help' them deal with situations and the effect of the drugs can vary from person to person. Many people see cannabis as a harmless substance that helps you to relax and be calm, but it can also be harmful and in some cases has been known to cause psychotic illnesses. One method of using cannabis is by smoking it mixed with tobacco – since smoking is banned on the majority of flights, the problem may start to escalate when the passenger is prevented from smoking.

- Mental health issues – there are a range of mental health issues which would not have any impact on a passenger flying to a destination, for example somebody with Down's

Level 2 Introduction to Cabin Crew

Syndrome. However, there are also conditions which can be exacerbated in the confines of an aircraft cabin, e.g. paranoia and schizophrenia. If a passenger is likely to be a potential hazard, or adversely affect the welfare and comfort of other passengers, the cabin crew would have to take action. Occasionally passengers act in an uncharacteristic way because of personal phobias, e.g. claustrophobia or aerophobia (the fear of flying)

Activity ➡

Read this story about a passenger who tried to open the door on a flight at 36,000 feet: http://www.dailymail.co.uk/news/article-2037731/Passenger-tries-open-plane-doors-36-000ft-screams-flight-simulator.html

6. Being able to deal with passengers

In dealing with any one of the incidents and conflict situations described in the previous section, it is important that the cabin crew follow company procedures meticulously, keep the flight crew informed, work as a team and remain calm. The cabin crew dealing with the situation should be confident and in control. Effective communication skills are important and body language should be used effectively. Other crew members should continue with service to other passengers, unless they are needed to assist in any way.

There is a chain of command when dealing with passenger incidents and conflicts, and this mirrors the chain of command used in emergency situations. When an incident occurs, any cabin crew member should feel empowered to deal with it. However, if the situation develops into conflict the incident will be referred upwards through the senior cabin crew and ultimately to the flight crew.

Level 2 Introduction to Cabin Crew

Did you know? The flight crew would not become physically involved in a conflict situation as they could be knocked out or injured. Their priority is to make a judgement based on the information they are given about the situation and, if necessary, divert the aircraft to the nearest airport where the offending passenger will be offloaded. Many airlines also carry 'restraint kits', which can be used to physically restrain the passenger in their seat. The Captain has to authorise the cabin crew to use this piece of equipment.

Activity →

Use the internet to research an incident which occurred on a flight from Manchester to Majorca on May 31 2012. Do you think the action the airline took was correct? Discuss this with a partner.

Cabin service - selling techniques

Introduction

One of the roles of cabin crew is to look after the welfare of their passengers and you will receive training on how to perform cabin service tasks effectively. Some people view the services that are offered as an opportunity for the airline to make money, but it is also an opportunity for you to offer a service to your passengers. As you welcome the passengers on board, you are preparing to look after them for the next hour, or hours, and part of this service includes offering them refreshments and an opportunity to buy goods.

Charter and budget airlines do use the sales of drinks, meals and snacks, as well as tax-free/duty-free goods, to generate income. You, as cabin crew, will be offered the incentive of commission on the sales and rewards if you exceed the sales target for the flight. Many scheduled airlines include the cost for the drinks and food in the ticket price, so their emphasis is on cabin service delivery. Scheduled airlines do, however, offer a range of tax-free/duty-free goods for passengers to purchase either on the flight or online.

This unit will help you to develop your knowledge and understanding of:

- Establishing rapport with passengers
- Discovering passengers' wants and needs
- On-board products and services
- Selling techniques
- Currency calculations
- How to provide a cabin service

Level 2 Introduction to Cabin Crew

Learning Outcomes	Assessment Criteria
1 Understand how to establish a rapport with passengers on board the aircraft	**1.1** Explain the importance of creating a positive image of the organisation to passengers **1.2** Explain how to meet and greet the passengers in a professional manner **1.3** Explain the importance of first impressions **1.4** Describe how body language can influence the relationships with passengers
2 Understand how to establish passengers' wants and needs	**2.1** Describe the difference between a customer's wants and needs **2.2** Describe the difference between open and closed questions and the benefits of both **2.3** Explain what is meant by active listening **2.4** Identify different types of non-verbal communication signals **2.5** Explain the importance of summarising the passenger's requirements
3 Know on board products and services	**3.1** Describe the procedures for a bar service **3.2** Describe the procedures for a meal/snack service **3.3** Describe the procedures for a tax-free/duty-free service **3.4** Describe the procedures for ancillary services
4 Understand selling techniques	**4.1** Describe selling techniques **4.2** Describe the difference between features and benefits of products and services **4.3** Describe the importance of merchandising
5 Be able to carry out currency calculations	**5.1** Identify a range of currencies used in popular destinations **5.2** Convert amounts from GBP to a range of currencies **5.3** Convert amounts from a range of currencies to GBP **5.4** Calculate change for passengers
6 Be able to provide a cabin service	**6.1** Provide a refreshment service **6.2** Provide a tax-free service

1. Establishing rapport with passengers

It is important that you establish a positive connection with your passengers. The relationship you establish at the first meeting will affect the passenger's perception of the airline, their confidence in you (should an emergency situation occur) and your job satisfaction. The first time your passengers may have observed you is on your journey through the airport terminal on the way to the aircraft. When you arrive for work you should be smart, well groomed, professional and confident. Wearing a uniform makes you noticeable – it is part of the airline identity – and that first impression needs to be positive.

The next occasion that the passenger sees you is when they board the aircraft. It is important to be ready for your passengers and that does not just mean standing at the door or in the cabin, but means:

- Looking smart
- Smiling
- Using open body language
- Having a friendly expression
- Giving a polite and cheerful greeting
- Giving brief directions to seats
- Assisting or arranging for assistance
- Being attentive

Not only does that initial greeting help each passenger to relax and to see the flight as an enjoyable experience, but it also enables the cabin crew to observe any potential problems, e.g. someone with bluish lips and having slight difficulty breathing, someone who looks frightened or who is distracted. It is also an opportunity to deliver that extra level of service by helping with a child's seatbelt or putting a bag in the overhead locker. On another level, cabin crew will also notice passengers who could be potential ABPs (able-bodied persons) who could be called upon in an emergency situation.

Did you know? First impressions are made within seconds of meeting someone and it is challenging to alter that judgement once it has been made. Therefore, make sure that it is always positive – treat people as you would like to be treated and in a professional manner. At the same time, do not confuse friendly with familiar.

Activity ➡

Stand in front of a mirror and smile. Does the smile light up your face or is it a token gesture. Stand with your arms crossed – what impression does this give? Try different greetings – why is it important to vary what you say?

The first impression that your passengers should have is of someone who is pleased to see them, someone who is prepared to help them and someone who is confident about what they are doing.

2. Establishing passenger needs and wants

Airline companies satisfy the basic needs of passengers by providing them with the necessary aspects related to their personal comfort and safety. On an aircraft, the passenger needs a seat to sit in, a seatbelt to keep them secure and someone who will check that the seatbelt is secure. These *needs* develop into *wants* when people are given the opportunity to make choices, for example choosing a seat with extra legroom, one that converts into a bed or an individual entertainment system.

> **Did you know?** Needs are what a person *must* have for survival, whereas wants are more personal and are what a person *would like to have*. For example, if a passenger asks for a drink of water, offering them a choice of bottled or tap water with or without ice enables them to state their preference. Offering the passenger a choice makes them feel valued and special.

Using 'open' and 'closed' questions helps cabin crew to respond to passenger requests, to develop opportunities to sell products and to find out information, e.g. in a medical situation.

Closed questions usually result in short answers and they can be used effectively in a number of situations. Closed questions can be answered with a 'yes' or 'no', but they can also be answered with a short phrase. Closed questions are useful when checking information and establishing facts. These questions are quick to answer, which might be

relevant if time is short, and it also means that the person asking the questions has more control over the conversation. *"Have you secured your seatbelt"* is an example of a closed question.

Open questions give cabin crew the opportunity to find out more information – they involve the listener and give the person more time to think about their answer. Open questions are useful when trying to find out details and preferences when you are asked to recommend a product. For example, a passenger may want to buy a gift of perfume for a friend, but they are not sure which fragrance to select. You could ask *"which fragrance has your friend used in the past?"* – this is an example of an open question. Using open questions gives control of the conversation to the respondent (the person answering the question). Open questions often begin with: which, what, why, how and describe.

Using a combination of open and closed questions is a valuable skill in selling products. It is equally important to listen carefully to responses and to show that you are listening. Acknowledge that you are listening by maintaining eye contact, nodding and developing the dialogue if a comment is made that you need more information on – this is known as 'active listening'. Once the conversation has been completed, it is useful to repeat back the key points of the information gathered to ensure that you offer the right product or solution.

Throughout any dialogue, non-verbal communication is a key factor. For example, if the goods you are selling are on a trolley which is slightly above the passenger eye level then present the product to them – sometimes the action of placing the product in their hands helps to close the sale.

Non-verbal communication (NVC), or body language, is all about the way we present ourselves to others and transmit messages, either intentionally or unintentionally. Banging the table to make a point, making eye contact, shrugging our shoulders or creating a particular facial expression are all examples of non-verbal communication.

Other common types of non-verbal communication include:

- Bodily contact – e.g. shaking somebody's hand or patting them on the back
- Physical proximity – the distance we feel we need to keep between ourselves and other people
- Orientation – where we place ourselves in relation to other people, e.g. the senior member of cabin crew may sit at the head of the table in a formal meeting
- Posture – whether slumped in a seat, sitting upright and straight or leaning against a wall, there is often something about our body posture that relays a message to those around us
- Gestures – e.g. giving a 'thumbs up' to show that all is well
- Facial expressions – smiling, crying and grimacing are just some of the many ways in which the face can transmit an enormous variety of emotions

Passengers should be made to feel welcome from the first moment they step on to the aircraft. Cabin crew should always smile and greet the customer in a friendly, polite and professional manner. Negative body language, such as crossed arms, ignoring the passenger, a lack of eye contact or a surly facial expression should be avoided at all times when carrying out cabin crew duties.

> **Did you know?** As cabin crew, it is necessary to be aware of the environment around you. For example, you may be in the process of selling an expensive watch to a passenger when someone with a small child needs you to move the trolley so that they can get access to the toilet… do you snatch the watch back, ignore the passenger with the child?
>
> In this situation, the best approach is to explain what you are going to do, politely take the watch back and place it on the trolley, and then return to the sale once you have manoeuvred to allow the parent and child to get to the toilet. You may choose to leave the watch with the passenger and that has to be a decision made on your judgement on the day.

3. On-board products and services

Airlines offer a range of services to meet the basic needs of passengers for food and drink. The service offered depends on the length of flight, the cost of the ticket and the 'product' the airline offers. For example, a budget airline operating short flights normally doesn't include any food or drink in the ticket price. Instead, a food and drinks service is offered by the cabin crew and passengers purchase their chosen items. A scheduled flight generally includes food within the ticket price, with the quantity and quality of food offered depending on the flight duration and the travel class.

During the pre-flight briefing, the senior member of cabin crew informs the cabin crew of the order of service for the flight. The cabin crew then work as a team to ensure that the service is delivered to the passengers in a professional and co-ordinated manner. The majority of aircraft have one galley at the front of the aircraft and another at the rear; some aircraft have one aisle while others have two, so it is important that service starts at the same time.

When the cabin crew board the aircraft, and after they have completed their safety and security checks, they check the catering equipment and start some of the preparations for a co-ordinated and efficient flight. The catering company will have loaded the carts containing meal trays, bar minerals and tax-free/duty-free goods onto the aircraft. There will also be a set of smaller metal boxes that contain glasses, replacement minerals and other dry goods required on the flight, e.g. coffee, tea bags, sugar and dried milk.

> **Did you know?** The coffee comes in a sachet that is opened and tipped into the coffee pot. When the cabin crew are ready to serve the hot drinks they pour on boiling water from the water boiler in the galley. Tea is made by using one large tea bag, which is placed into the pot, and then boiling water is added. Some airlines offer individual drinks and these often come in smaller servings or in pre-prepared cups, which are served as required.

An aircraft galley (kitchen) is a confined space and it is essential to keep it tidy and clean. Every item has its designated stowage and it is important to return items to the correct location. The galleys are often located on an emergency exit route, making it essential that every item must be returned to its correct location with the retaining clips in place for take-off and landing.

Level 2 Introduction to Cabin Crew

> **Did you know?** The retaining clips used in the galley are red. On the carts (under the work surface) there are two clips, one being longer than the other. During normal flight it is possible to use the smaller clip only, but for take-off and landing both clips must be used for extra safety. The carts contain many heavy items and if not properly stowed they could cause a lot of damage and injury. Some of the containers are at head height and should never be left open – closing container doors and putting carts back becomes second nature to all cabin crew over time.

After take-off the seals can be removed from the tax-free/duty-free carts in preparation for cabin service.

Seals are placed on carts for a number of reasons. Firstly, as a security measure to ensure that no unauthorised person is able to place any suspect item in the cart. Secondly, to meet HMRC (HM Revenue and Customs) regulations, which restrict selling tax-free/duty-free goods until the aircraft is airborne. Lastly, seals are used to prevent theft.

Seals are placed on the carts before they leave the secure area where they have been packed. The carts are sealed again before landing overseas and on return to the UK.

Different colour seals are used for outbound and inbound flights, while some airlines use a different colour for catering supplies.

After take-off, and once the seatbelt sign has been switched off, the senior cabin crew member makes an announcement informing passengers of the bar/beverage service. While this announcement is being made, the rest of the cabin crew prepare the carts for the service, making sure that the ice bucket is full, lemon slices are available, sufficient glasses are stacked and the display on the top of the cart is attractive, for example by placing a couple of wine bottles on the top of a drinks cart to encourage passengers to purchase wine to have with their meal. Cabin crew should carry a float with them to give change for goods purchased; usually the No. 1 and No. 2 are responsible for providing the float and ensuring it is removed during the post-flight cashing up.

The process of delivering the bar service can vary from airline to airline and aircraft to aircraft. During initial training, service standards are taught and operating cabin crew will be reminded during their pre-flight briefing. If two cabin crew members are operating a cart then

a system of leaving two rows for the person on the galley side of the cart starts the service effectively, but do remember to communicate with passengers who may think they have been missed out.

> **Did you know?** The brakes on the carts operate from either end – do not have your toes under the edge of the cart or you may get hurt when your partner presses the green lever to move on!

As the service progresses through the cabin and the cart needs replenishing the person on the galley side could return to get more supplies or, if there is a crew member in the galley, ringing the call bell and holding up the item in short supply will indicate that you need more of that item on the cart.

As with all services, the product delivery needs to be efficient and professional, for example never placing mineral cans or bottles in the glass and always offering ice and lemon if appropriate for the drink. Place the drink on the table and, if you drop a mineral can, replace it otherwise it will explode when opened. Do not have a social conversation with your colleague – remember that the passenger is the customer and you are there to make their flight an enjoyable experience.

When the bar service has been completed and preparations are being made for the meal service, cabin crew collect any debris from the passengers. This may be completed using a tray or there may be a waste cart which will be taken through the cabin to collect items.

Members of cabin crew will now prepare to serve the meals. Hot meals are available on the majority of flights and the menu will depend on the airline choice. Some companies have adopted the practice of offering snacks and quick bites rather than the set menu previously available on charter flights, meaning that passengers can make their personal choice. On scheduled flights, an extensive menu is available across the different travel classes. In general, passengers will be given a hot meal on a tray which has been set up with a cup, cutlery pack with salt, pepper, sugar and milk included.

The hot meals are prepared and chilled in a catering unit, transported to the aircraft and loaded into the ovens on board. When required, the meals are reheated, checked with a

probe to ensure they are cooked to the correct temperature and placed in a container which is put on top of the meal cart. The cart is then taken out into the cabin and the cabin crew take out the set up tray, place the hot meal onto the tray and pass the tray to the passenger. It is important to present the tray so that the passengers do not burn themselves with the hot dish, and so that it is in the correct position ready for the passenger to begin eating.

Did you know? If a passenger is travelling with a small child, the cabin crew should offer to hold their meal back until the child has eaten. Take extra care when handing out meals to elderly people since they may not be able to grip the tray – put it onto their tray table to avoid any spillage.

Once the meals have been distributed the coffee service begins. Remember that the water for the drinks is very hot, so always have a cloth ready to mop up any spillages. Take a small tray and ask the passenger to place the cup on it. Offer tea if people would prefer and orange squash for the children.

Throughout the drinks and meals service it is important to maintain hygiene standards, by keeping surfaces wiped down, washing hands frequently or using hand wash gel. If you have to clean any spillage always use protective gloves.

Did you know? Some airlines give staff disposable gloves to wear when they are collecting the meal trays after passengers have finished eating.

During the pre-flight briefing, cabin crew are given information about any dietary requests that passengers have made when they booked. Generally, the passenger location will be made known to the cabin crew by the ground handling agent who will know the seat number allocation.

Activity ➡

Use the internet to help you to decode the following meal requirements:

GFML, DBML, SFML, LSML, RVML, VLML.

When the passengers have finished their meal the cabin crew collect the used trays and place them back into the catering cart. Any half-drunk cups of coffee or tea are placed in a metal tray on top of the trolley so that they can be emptied before being thrown away. Once the cart is loaded with the used trays it is returned to the correct stowage in the galley ready to be removed and replaced during the aircraft turnaround.

Now that the passengers' basic needs for food and drink have been met the cabin crew start to offer the sale of tax-free/duty-free items. In the past, passengers who travelled on a flight were able to purchase a limited amount of goods duty-free – this meant that the goods were cheaper than buying the same product in the UK. The goods were cheaper because they did not have the cost of excise duty (tax) added to the basic cost. However, in July 1999 changes were made to flights within the European Union and people were unable to buy alcohol and tobacco at the reduced prices, although the amount of these products that they could buy was increased. Items such as fragrances, cosmetics, skin care products, photographic and electrical goods, jewellery and souvenirs are sold at a tax-free price (which means they are exempt from VAT). On fights outside of the EU passengers can purchase duty-free goods, but the amount of purchases is limited.

Activity ➡

Visit this website to familiarise yourself with duty-free and tax-free sales and allowances for airline passengers:

www.gov.uk/duty-free-goods

71

Before the tax-free/duty-free service begins, the senior member of cabin crew will make an announcement preparing passengers for the service, mentioning the in-flight magazine which gives details of the range of goods available to purchase on board. They will also give details of any special promotions on the flight and remind passengers of the methods of payment that can be used.

While this announcement is being delivered, the rest of the cabin crew prepare the carts for the service. Presenting a good visual display will stimulate passenger interest, which will encourage them to look at what is available and enable cabin crew to develop sales opportunities for which they may earn commission.

Airline services do differ, but generally there will be carts with the alcohol and tobacco products and other carts containing the perfume and gift range. The service delivery will depend on the aircraft configuration, flight destination, passenger type and departure airport, e.g. if you have a flight departing from Gatwick and passengers have already had the opportunity to spend time in the airport shops before the flight, your sales may be reduced.

Some airlines, especially low-cost operators such as Ryanair and easyJet, make extra profits from selling ancillary products/services on board, for example bus and train tickets for onward travel, car hire and even lottery tickets!

4. Selling techniques

Each individual has their own approach to selling products, but it is important that they also have the flexibility and ability to adapt their style to ensure a successful sale. From the first moment the passenger boarded the flight, the cabin crew have been developing a rapport and it is important to build on this positive relationship by offering a professional service. Passengers are a captive audience, but it is important not to use aggressive sales techniques or to make false claims. This may work in the short-term, but when the passenger has time to reflect they may develop negative feelings about the airline.

The starting point for the sales service is the PA (public address) system. Announcements are usually scripted by the company and contain the basic information required. Remember that delivery technique is important and the tone should be interesting and upbeat. If there is a special promotional offer then tell passengers about it. Individual cabin crew members may be more accomplished at selling than others – use their skills to help the whole team achieve sales targets. Sales training now forms a key part of the initial cabin service course. Additional promotional events are hosted by suppliers and the airline in-flight service managers arrange workshops and seminars to develop cabin crew sales skills.

It is important that the salesperson (the cabin crew member) has excellent product knowledge. They need to be able to answer any questions that the passengers may ask. If a particular fragrance is not available cabin crew need to be able to offer an alternative. Using open questions will help cabin crew to discover what the passengers are looking for. Crew should be able to give advice on the suitability of a product and know the features and

benefits of a range of products. For example, a *feature* of a fragrance may be that it contains a variety of essential oils. The *benefit* of this could be that the users skin will remain soft and supple. When selling products and services it is important to present both features and (particularly) benefits to have the best chance of closing a sale.

With the change in legislation mentioned earlier, which has altered the duty-free perception, it is important that airlines are able to offer alternative products which offer financial savings for passengers. The sales of tobacco and alcohol on flights are not as high as they once were and airlines responded positively by extending the range of cosmetics and gifts, which are VAT exempt. The airline in-flight marketing department will monitor trends, look at what their competitors offer, study their passenger profiles, flight destinations and provide the cabin crew with a range of suitable products.

> **Did you know?** Many airlines offer a buy-before-you-fly service for duty-free/tax-free goods, with airport duty-free shops and airlines displaying their products on line.

5. Currency calculations

One of the skills that cabin crew need to demonstrate is numeracy. On a typical flight, they will be handling money, giving change, converting sterling to currency, currency to sterling, calculating opening and closing stocks, commission payments and banking bar takings at the end of the flight.

Many airlines set the currency conversion rate every month and cabin crew are expected to ensure that they have the correct currency rate. On-board computers will be programmed to assist with currency conversions and completing calculations, including how much change or additional payment is required.

Level 2 Introduction to Cabin Crew

> **Did you know?** Much of the stocktaking process on board is computerised, but cabin crew still need to know how to "*count a bar*" should the system fail, e.g. when counting cartons of 200 cigarettes the amount is expressed as 10 because in one carton of 200 cigarettes there are 10 individual packs of 20. Bottles are counted as 1. On the stocktaking form (the bar control form) will be listed opening stock (the goods you started with) and closing stock (the items that you have left).

Although calculators and computers make the process easier it is still essential that cabin crew understand the concept of currency conversion and are familiar with the formulas used.

> **Did you know?** Any change is always given to passengers in sterling. Cabin crew cannot sell currency to passengers – this would be illegal.

To change sterling (UK currency) to foreign money you would multiply by the exchange rate. For example, if £1 equals €1.19 and you have £100 to change you should receive 100 x 1.19 = €119. On a flight you would more likely be changing the Euros back to sterling and in this case you would divide the foreign money by the exchange rate. As an example, if a passenger has to pay £22 for a perfume, and they wish to use the €15 they have left and pay the balance in sterling, you would have to change the €15 into sterling. To do this, you divide the Euros by the rate of exchange, so €15 ÷1.19 = £12.60. Once you have this amount you take it away from the amount owed, i.e. £22.00 - £12.60 = £9.40. Therefore, the passenger needs to pay another £9.40 in sterling to complete the transaction.

> **Activity** ➡
>
> If you found these calculations confusing, or you do not feel confident about your numeracy skills, then you need to practise. Part of the interview process to become cabin crew may involve a numeracy test. Use a website such as BBC *Bitesize* to find out more about foreign exchange calculations.

The airline industry is a very competitive market, with airlines continually developing ways of exceeding passenger expectations. For airlines to be successful, the workforce must be responsive and demonstrate their commitment at all times. During the cabin crew selection process, the recruitment team will be looking for indicators that you can deliver excellent customer care and enhance the passenger experience. They will be looking for a range of skills and competencies.

6.   Providing a cabin service

We discussed earlier in this unit the stages that cabin crew go through when delivering an effective service for passengers (see from page 66). On a typical short-haul flight the cabin service follows this pattern:

1.   Serving drinks and snacks
2.   Food service
3.   Selling duty-free and tax-free goods
4.   Offering any ancillary products/services

On longer flights there is more time for the cabin crew to deliver the cabin service, which may vary from the pattern shown above and include more stages depending on the flight length.

Activity ➡

Visit the British Airways website to research the travel classes available on flights, noting the meal options and the other facilities available in each class.

Using the easyJet website, find out what food and drink options are offered to passengers.

Visit the Thomson Airways website and research the in-flight services available to passengers, including food and drink.

Draw up a chart that compares the different food and drink options offered by these 3 airlines. What differences do you notice? Are there any similarities? What factors do you think influence the products and services offered by each airline?

75

Procedures such as serving drinks and food must be carried out efficiently, while not losing account of the fact that every passenger is an individual and has their own specific needs. They may also need help with other aspects of the flight, for example with using the entertainment systems, finding out about onward travel and other flight connections.

Many of the skills needed to succeed as a member of cabin crew are honed over time, with newer staff members often learning from their more experienced colleagues.

Making passenger announcements on board an aircraft

Introduction

Communicating with passengers is one of the key aspects of a successful flight, whether it is to inform the passengers about sales and service, e.g. *"the cabin crew will shortly be coming into the cabin with a bar service...."* or to give the passengers information about safety procedures, e.g. *"in the unlikely event of a sudden loss of pressure..."* The ability of cabin crew to deliver the information effectively and appropriately is very important. Most of the announcements they are required to give will be over the public address (PA) system using a script, but sometimes it may be necessary for cabin crew to communicate without a script or the PA system.

This unit will help you to develop your knowledge and understanding of:

- The communication techniques used on board
- How to use the PA system
- The correct methods to use to ensure successful communication
- Passenger announcements used during normal flight operations
- Passenger announcements made during emergency situations

Learning Outcomes	Assessment Criteria
1 Know how to use passenger announcements during a flight	**1.1** Describe communication techniques for passenger announcements **1.2** Identify the methods to communicate passenger announcements effectively in different situations **1.3** Describe passenger announcements that are used during a normal flight **1.4** Describe passenger announcements that are required for emergency situations
2 Be able to make passenger announcements	**2.1** Carry out passenger announcements that are used during a normal flight **2.2** Carry out passenger announcements that are used for emergency situations

1. Know how to use passenger announcements during a flight

Communication techniques for passenger announcements

When you communicate with someone you are essentially conveying a message. We saw in Unit 5 the importance of *non-verbal* communication and how it can be used effectively. With *verbal* communication you need to think about the techniques you can use to deliver information and the importance of a number of factors, including:

- Pace – if you race through the information it is impossible for the people listening to fully understand what you are telling them, but if you talk too slowly people get bored and may not give you their full attention.

- Pitch – this is about the quality of the sounds you produce and how these can affect the delivery of information. For example, when people become frightened, the pitch of their voice often becomes higher. Lowering the pitch of your voice can make your message more persuasive, which is great for selling those tax-free/duty-free items on board and increasing your commission!

- Volume – the volume of your delivery can be affected by external factors and situations, e.g. during normal flight operations there is always a background noise coming from the aircraft engines. Occasionally, you may have a group of passengers who are excited and who talk very loudly. In an emergency situation you may have to make yourself heard over screams, mechanical noises and sirens.

Level 2 Introduction to Cabin Crew

> **Did you know?** Volume is just not about shouting, but more about projecting your voice. If you shout you can sound emotional and out of control, but if you project your voice loudly you will sound confident and in control. In an emergency situation you are instructed to "*shout*" commands – these will need to be heard above all of the external noises, the internal panic and screaming, and by the passengers 10 rows away from you.

- Diction and pronunciation – this is about your style of speaking, the words you choose and how you express them.

> ## Activity ➡
>
> Read out the following arrival announcement: "*Ladies and gentlemen, welcome to Luton Airport*". Did you sound the "T" in the word Luton or did you arrive at Lu'on Airport? Which sounds more professional?

Methods of communication

The public address (PA) system on the aircraft allows the flight deck and cabin crew to make passenger announcements which can be heard throughout the passenger cabin, the galley areas and in the toilets. The system is incorporated into the communication handset at crew stations (the seats where cabin crew sit for take-off and landing) and can be used at a number of locations. Generally, the senior cabin crew member is responsible for the delivery of passenger announcements and, in many airlines, there is also a pre-recorded system which can be programmed to deliver certain key announcements in different languages. If there should be a failure of the PA system, alternative methods of communication can be used, e.g. a loud hailer or shouted instructions.

As cabin crew you will be required to use the PA system to give passengers information, using scripts produced by the airline. There are 2 types of passenger announcements:

- Safety-related – these scripts are written to meet CAA regulations and to ensure consistency and compliance. The style of delivery should reflect the serious nature of the content. The pre-take off demonstration gives important information which could affect the survival of passengers in an emergency situation. For example, if an explosive decompression occurs there may be no time for the cabin crew to explain how to put the mask on.

- Service-related – there is more flexibility with this type of announcement and the No.1 member of cabin crew may allow junior members of the crew to deliver their own passenger announcements, perhaps concerning a tax-free promotion on that day. However, professional standards still need to be maintained and the airline reputation could be damaged by an inappropriate delivery or false statements, e.g. telling a passenger that a watch is guaranteed to be waterproof to a depth of 100m when in actual fact it is not.

Passenger announcements used during a normal flight

There are a number of passenger announcements made during a normal flight. As the passengers board the aircraft they are advised to place their hand luggage in the overhead lockers and, in certain situations, they may be requested to take their seats quickly to avoid delaying the flight.

Once the passengers are seated and the final paperwork is being completed, the senior member of cabin crew welcomes the passengers on board the aircraft. During this initial passenger announcement the flight number and destination will be mentioned – this is an opportunity to ensure that all passengers are on the correct flight before the doors are closed for take-off.

> **Did you know?** It is very unusual for passengers to get on the wrong aircraft, but it has been known to happen. On 30 June 2012 a passenger boarded a flight for Malmo in Sweden instead of his intended destination of Biarritz in France!

After the aircraft doors have been closed, and the aircraft is positioning for take-off, the senior cabin crew member will welcome the passengers on board on behalf of the captain and give the introduction to the passenger safety briefing. It is important to gain the passenger's attention to this particular demonstration because of the safety information that is being given. On some flights the safety demonstration will be a video and on other flights it will be a manual demonstration by the cabin crew.

> **Did you know?** There are a number of video safety demonstrations on YouTube. When you watch these you will see the different methods used by airlines to ensure passengers pay attention. A manual demonstration is useful in that it gives the crew delivering the demonstration an opportunity to observe the passengers and their reactions.

After the 'fasten seatbelt' sign has been switched off, the No. 1 will remind passengers about the 'no smoking' rule, advise them to keep their seatbelts loosely fastened and inform them

Level 2 Introduction to Cabin Crew

of the services, bar service, meals and tax-free/duty-free goods that they will be offered on the flight. During this passenger announcement, information about the in-flight entertainment system and the passenger call bell location will be given and reference may be made to the in-flight magazine.

> **Did you know?** Many airlines have in-flight magazines in the seat pocket in front of passengers. Some hand out (and collect in) the magazines on every flight. The growth in new technology means that this information may be available on the display screen in front of the passenger.

Electronic devices can now be used on board aircraft, but there are restrictions and the cabin crew will inform passengers when they are allowed to switch their devices on. During the flight the pilot may also use the PA system to give information about the route and any other details that may be of interest to the passengers.

> **Did you know?** It is important that the cabin crew listen to the flight crew announcements. If the pilot mentions a tail wind it could mean that the flight time has become shorter and the cabin crew will have less time to complete the service.
>
> Passengers often ask "*where are we*?", and cabin crew can make an informed guess from the information given by the pilot.
>
> The pilot may mention turbulence, which could affect the time at which the cabin crew serve hot drinks.

On the approach into the destination airport the senior member of cabin crew makes a PA announcement to ensure that the passenger cabin is prepared for landing – passengers must return to their seats, seatbacks and seat tables to be in the upright position, hand luggage securely stowed and seatbelts fastened. Remember that most aircraft accidents happen on take-off and landing, so these preparations ensure that, if an emergency evacuation was required, all escape routes would be clear.

On arrival at the destination airport, and as the aircraft is taxiing on to stand, the No. 1 gives information about the destination, for example the temperature and local time. Personal safety information is also given, e.g. "*do not undo your seatbelts until the sign has been switched off and the aircraft has come to a standstill*" and "*no smoking until you are in a designated smoking area*", plus a final comment on behalf of the company and airline, such as "*we wish you an enjoyable holiday*" and/or "*we look forward to you flying with us again in the future*".

> **Did you know?** The content of the final announcement depends on the type of flight operation, i.e. charter flight = enjoyable holiday, scheduled flight = information about facilities at the airport, low-cost airlines = information about onward travel.
>
> Whichever airline you are working for, this last announcement and your "*farewell*" will be the last opportunity you have to make a positive impression on the passengers.

Passenger announcements during emergency situations

The approach and delivery of passenger announcements in an emergency situation needs to be confident and calming. There *may* be time to deliver a scripted passenger announcement or the situation may need a quick response and shouted instructions – think about the planned and unplanned emergency situations we discussed in Unit 3 (see from page 35 onwards).

In a planned emergency the captain will have given the NITS briefing and advised the cabin crew of the time available. Their EPB (emergency procedures booklet) will include alternative passenger announcements to use, depending on the amount of time available.

In an unplanned emergency there will be no time to search for the correct passenger announcement and the cabin crew will need to react using their initiative. For example, in an explosive decompression the most important actions would be to ensure that every passenger is in a seat and that they have activated their drop-down oxygen mask. It is also important to make sure that all passengers have their seatbelts on and securely fastened. The announcements given by the cabin crew should cover these emergency procedures as a matter of urgency.

> **Did you know?** In an explosive decompression, the cabin crew would sit in the first available seat and grab the oxygen mask – they would not return to their crew stations, where the PA system is located.

Once the aircraft has reached a safe altitude, the senior member of cabin crew would give a post-decompression passenger announcement to reassure and inform the passengers of the flight crew intentions.

When making a passenger announcement in an emergency situation, the content of the message and the delivery may need to be modified to ensure passenger compliance:

Level 2 Introduction to Cabin Crew

- In the case of a bomb threat the passenger announcements need to be delivered in a calm, authoritative manner, giving clear instructions on actions that must be taken.

- In the case of a medical incident on board, a passenger announcement may be made asking for assistance from a medically qualified person. The announcement may need to be repeated and certain words stressed, e.g. medically qualified doctor, nurse or paramedic.

- In a planned emergency situation, and when the aircraft has landed, the cabin crew begin the evacuation process and shout instructions to passengers to get them off the aircraft as quickly as possible. They will give short, positive commands, repeating the sequence to keep a steady flow of passengers. The delivery will be fast-paced to encourage a speedy evacuation and instructions should be directed to people at least 5 rows back as well as those at the exit to ensure passengers are prepared for the evacuation slide.

- In a planned emergency ditching, i.e. a landing on water, there may be more time to evacuate the passengers and the pace of delivery and the instructions will be varied. The passenger announcement system may not be available, but a megaphone (or loud hailer) could be used.

- Severe turbulence is very unusual, but it can happen without any prior warning. In this situation the cabin crew may need to shout instructions to passengers to give them commands about the action to take. This type of situation needs an immediate reaction, so cabin crew need to use assertive tones to communicate with passengers, giving them clear instructions as to what to do. Once the situation is under control the flight crew will make an announcement to reassure passengers.

2. Be able to make passenger announcements

People are often nervous about using a PA (public address system) and do not like the sound of their voice when they hear it played back. The best advice is to practise, read out aloud and think about the relevance of the message:

- Are you trying to sell something? Use persuasive, pleasant tones and smile while talking.

- If it is an emergency situation and you want people to do as you say without question, be assertive, use short phrases and be concise.

When using the PA as a member of cabin crew, you must:

1. Be prepared, take time to have your script in front of you, prepare yourself mentally and remember to breathe at appropriate times

2. Concentrate on what you are reading and use pause, pace, pitch and diction to keep the passenger's attention

3. Be confident in your delivery

4. Smile – especially for service-related announcements. It may seem strange, but the action of smiling while you talk makes you sound friendly and professional.

Good communication skills are an essential aspect of being cabin crew; the way that you deliver the message could affect the outcome.

Activity ➡

Record yourself reading a piece of information. On the first occasion do not smile as you read. Now read the same information again, this time with a smile. Can you hear the difference? Remember on a PA your voice will be amplified.

Glossary of common terms used by cabin crew

24-hour clock: developed to avoid confusion about a.m. and p.m. Always written as four figures and when the time does not have four figures a zero is added, e.g. one thirty in the morning is written as 0130, while one thirty in the afternoon is written as 1330.

2-letter codes: airlines use 2-letter codes to identify the company, for example BA – British Airways and MT – Thomas Cook. These letters usually precede numbers and are used to compile the flight numbers found on all documentation relating to a flight, e.g. BA035.

3-letter codes: these are used to designate airports. Some codes are easily recognisable, e.g. EDI – Edinburgh and LBA – Leeds Bradford, while others are less obvious, e.g. Cardiff – CWL and Birmingham – BHX

ABPs: stands for able-bodied passengers, who may be called on to help the cabin crew in the event of an emergency evacuation on an aircraft. Certain passengers would **not** be suitable as ABPs, for example nervous flyers and pregnant women.

A/C: stands for aircraft and is used in written reports, e.g. 'Late arrival of IB A/C due to bad weather in GVA.'

Aerophobia: this is the fear of flying.

Air bridge: this is the piece of equipment that connects an aircraft to the terminal so that passengers can board and disembark in comfort and not be affected by the weather.

Air Navigation Order (ANO): the Air Navigation Order contains information about the day-to-day operation of the aviation industry. The focus of the CAA is to ensure safe air travel and they use legislation (international, European and domestic) to update and produce the ANO. This publication sets the standards for recruitment, training and procedures within all aspects of the aviation industry.

Airside: is the part of the airport that passengers can access with a valid boarding card and ticket, after going through passport control, ticket check and security. The duty-free/tax-free shops are located in this area. Only staff with a valid ID pass and security clearance can access this area. This term also refers to the general areas outside the airport building, but inside the perimeter fence, e.g. the ramp, the hangars, the aircraft stands, etc.

Arming: when cabin crew talk about 'arming' a door, they mean that the escape slide is now ready to be used when the door is opened should an emergency evacuation be needed.

ATC: stands for air traffic control. This group of people are responsible for guiding the aircraft through airspace and on the ground at airports. In the UK the CAA is responsible for regulating this service, which is responsible for safety in the air. No aircraft can take off without clearance from ATC personnel.

ATD: stands for actual time of departure. This is the time that is recorded on the paperwork when the aircraft takes off.

85

Bulkhead: this is a partition within the aircraft cabin, and also found in other areas such as the hold, to create rigidity and structure.

CAA: stands for Civil Aviation Authority, the UK organisation that is responsible for air safety and air traffic control.

Chain of command: the declared lines of authority on an aircraft that set out staff responsibilities. The Captain has ultimate responsibility for a flight and the senior member of cabin crew is responsible for the customer service issues.

Charter flight: a charter flight is one where a tour operator contracts an aircraft for a given period of time, e.g. to provide flights for package holidays to Mediterranean destinations over a summer season.

Chocks: these are triangular blocks, which are placed in front of and behind the aircraft wheels to prevent it from rolling forward or backward.

Dangerous goods: substances and equipment used on board an aircraft that could cause damage to health, property or the surrounding environment.

Day and month codes: abbreviated to the first 3 letters* or numbers can be used, e.g. the 1st of December 2014 would be 01DEC14. The abbreviated form is used on flight documents such as flight reports. *Days of the week may sometimes be written using the first 2 letters.

Daylight saving time: most countries in the world use daylight saving time (DST), which extends daylight artificially. The length of daylight hours changes with the seasons in the UK, with the longest days in the summer months. At 2 points in the year we move the clock on or back one hour to give us more daylight time. Other countries do the same, but the dates for changing may vary from the UK so for about one week the time differences may be non-standard.

Decompression: any loss of aircraft cabin pressure is known as decompression. The internal cabin altitude starts to increase to that of the actual flight altitude, oxygen supplies reduce and hypoxia (a shortage of oxygen in the body blood cells) can occur. Aircraft decompression can be rapid or slow.

Disarming: this term relates to the aircraft doors and the exit slide. When the door is in the disarmed mode it means that the evacuation slide will not inflate and the door can be opened for the passengers to disembark using the steps or an air bridge.

Disembarkation: the process of passengers departing from an aircraft.

Ditching: refers to an unplanned emergency landing on water.

Elapsed flying time: this is the actual time an aircraft spends in the air. It does not include time spent on the ground during turnaround, stopovers or taxiing. If you want to calculate flight time you need to remember that there are 60 minutes in one hour. For example, if you leave LHR at 1300GMT and arrive in ALC at 1530GMT the flight time is 2 hours 30 minutes and to give the local time you need to remember ALC time will be 1 hour ahead, so the local time will be 1530 + 0100 = 1630.

Level 2 Introduction to Cabin Crew

ETA: stands for estimated time of arrival. It is be used to give people an idea of when an aircraft might land, but it is only a guideline.

Flight crew: these are the pilots who fly the aircraft. There are usually 2 pilots – the Captain and a First Officer – although on long-haul trips there may be more.

Flight deck: the front part of an aircraft where the pilots are located.

Fuselage: this is the main body of the aircraft – the cylinder to which the wings and tail are attached.

Galley: is the kitchen area of the aircraft. Galleys can be located at both the front and back of the cabin. Some of the larger aircraft may use other locations. The catering equipment, ovens, water boilers and carts are all located in this area.

Gash bag: a term used to describe a rubbish bag used on an aircraft.

GMT: standing for Greenwich Mean Time (sometimes referred to as UTC – Universal Time Constant), GMT was developed to standardise time throughout the world. By using GMT people can use the same date, time, hour and minute to co-ordinate their activities. This does not mean that every country has the same time, but that it can be calculated using GMT as the constant. The world is divided into time zones.

Ground staff: these are members of staff who provide support services to an airline, e.g. dispatchers, baggage loaders, etc.

Hold: the area of the aircraft where the luggage is loaded, usually accessed on the lower, right-hand side of the fuselage. The luggage may be hand loaded or loaded in containers (depending on the size of aircraft). The front hold is usually pressurised and live animals can be transported in this hold area.

IATA: stands for International Air Transport Association, a trade body that represents most world airlines. Its primary aim is to promote safe, regular and economic air travel.

I/B: this abbreviation (which stands for inbound) is used when an aircraft is on the return sector of a flight, i.e. returning to the base airport or country of departure.

Jump seat: the name given to the cabin crew seats that are located adjacent to main emergency exit routes on an aircraft. These seats are referred to as 'jump seats' because they flip up (like a cinema seat) to make sure emergency exit routes are free from obstructions at all times.

Landside: this term refers to the parts of an airport that can be accessed by anybody, including people without a ticket for travel. On entry to a country, and once passengers have passed through customs control, they will exit into this part of the airport. *See also airside.*

Mission statement: a brief explanation of a company's fundamental purpose, e.g. '*to be the UK's most profitable airline*'.

NITS: this mnemonic stands for: **N** = Nature of the emergency; **I** = Intention, e.g. what action the Captain will be taking; **T** = Time, e.g. how much time until landing; **S** = Special

Level 2 Introduction to Cabin Crew

instructions, e.g. evacuate using left side only. It is used by cabin crew and flight crew in the event of an emergency situation on board an aircraft.

Offload: to take someone, or something, off an aircraft. A disruptive passenger, for example, may be offloaded at an airport and handed over to the police.

PA: stands for public address system. On aircraft, the PA is used to communicate with passengers, e.g. to announce the start of the safety demonstration. Sometimes the term PA is used to refer to the document which is read over the system.

Passenger cabin: the section of the aircraft that contains the passenger seats.

Passenger manifest: a list of the passengers on a flight.

PAX: this is the plural term for passengers – one passenger is referred to as a PAP. It is used in written documents and also during conversations between crew members.

PBE: stands for protective breathing equipment, such as a smoke hood, which cabin crew wear when fighting a fire on board an aircraft. Without this, cabin crew can be overcome by toxic smoke and fumes within 15-20 seconds. The PBE also protects the wearer from flames and heat which can cause damage to eyes and skin.

Phonetic alphabet: a series of words used to represent the letters of the alphabet in radio or telecommunications. The words are used to ensure that there is no confusion over which letter of the alphabet is being used, e.g. F and S can sound the same but Foxtrot and Sierra are very different. Approved by the International Civil Aviation Organisation and used worldwide.

Pilot incapacitation: the sudden inability of a pilot to continue flying an aircraft, usually caused by a medical emergency. The pilot who is not incapacitated will normally divert to the nearest available airport for landing.

PPE: stands for personal protective equipment, such as disposable gloves. One of the basic procedures is to provide personal protective equipment (PPE) for employees. The COSHH Regulations state that it is the employer's responsibility to provide, replace and pay for any PPE that is needed.

Protocols: these are rules and regulations laid down by airlines and regulators (such as the CAA) to ensure that passengers and crew have safe, secure and pleasant flights at all times.

Pushback: an aircraft does not have the facility to move backwards under its own power. A low-level, powerful vehicle called a tug with a tow bar is used to push the aircraft back from the stand onto the route for the taxiway. Once in position the aircraft can use engine power to move itself forward. Pushback is the name given to this procedure.

Risk assessment: this is a structured process used in health & safety to identify potential risks in the workplace and list measures that should be carried out to minimise these risks.

Level 2 Introduction to Cabin Crew

Roster: the work schedule that cabin crew are given to show which flights they are operating on which days. Cabin crew generally know which flights they will be operating at least a month in advance.

Scheduled flight: this is a flight that operates to a published timetable and offers seat-only sales. *See also charter flight.*

Sector: a flight is made up of a number of sectors – the period between take-off and landing. Therefore, a return flight to PMI from LTN will usually be 2 sectors. Long-haul flights sometimes consist of more sectors because of the distance travelled, although short-haul flights to more than one destination could incorporate a number of sectors.

SEP: stands for Safety and Emergency Procedures – a vital aspect of the cabin crew role. After initial training, cabin crew are constantly checked on their SEP knowledge during pre-flight briefings and an annual SEP exam. CAA inspectors may board any flight and check crew knowledge. The CAA also spot check completed SEP papers and monitor airline training programmes.

Slot: aircraft are allocated a take-off time by air traffic control. This time is given to ensure safety regulations related to aircraft separation rules. Sometimes flight crew have to negotiate another slot time if there is a problem with weather, late arrival of passengers or a technical fault.

Stand: the name given to the parking area that planes use at airports.

Stowage: the areas in the galley (kitchen) of an aircraft where items are stored so as to secure them for take-off and landing.

Time zones: the world is divided into 24 one-hour time zones based on lines of longitude. Some of the larger continents have more than one time zone, e.g. Australia and the United States of America. Time zone boundaries can be irregular depending on the country in question.

Turbulence: this is unexpected movement of an aircraft caused by a number of conditions, usually related to weather, but also a range of other situations affecting air flow. Severe turbulence can cause injury to passengers and crew.

U/S: stands for unserviceable and usually relates to a piece of equipment that has a defect and cannot be used, e.g. a cart with a faulty brake may have a label tied to it to notify the catering department. U/S is also used in relation to emergency equipment, e.g. an exit route becoming blocked.

UTC: *see GMT*

Zulu: this expression is used to denote zero time, which is the time at the Greenwich Meridian (in London) from which other times around the world are calculated. For example, if it is 1300 in London it will be 1400 in Paris – as you travel east you add time – but in New York it will be 0800 – as you travel west you take time away.

Level 2 Introduction to Cabin Crew